Knowmad Society

EDITED BY JOHN W. MORAVEC

Education Futures

This is a book.

But, it is not quite finished.

It needs your extra love and attention to grow even more. Make this book yours: Write and draw on it, highlight the parts you like, and tear out what you don't like.

Customize it, and build it into your own guide to Knowmad Society. Then, please share alike and pass this book on to someone else.

If you would like to share your ideas with us, please send them to info@knowmadsociety.com. We would love to hear from you!

Everybody reads books differently, so we built this one to be read in different ways.

If you're interested in what we have to say, but don't have time to read it all, don't worry. *We added summaries.*

If you like to scan for ideas before delving deeper, *we summarized many of our best ideas with short, sound bite-like quotes.*

So start now!
Write your own title here ↓

Contents

FOOD FOR THOUGHT
START CHEWING HERE

HOW CAN YOU APPROACH A PROJ

HAVE A TEAMBUILDING ACTIVITY
(or SIMPLY TEAM TALK) WHENEVER
• you are stuck as a team
• you disagree
• are losing focus or info on the way...

① ENT
• meet client
• set goals with client

② TEAM
☐ meet team
☐ team building
☐ communication guidelines

③ GOALs
☐ set goals in team
☐ set expectations (personal ...)

④ ACT
☐ lis

☐ def of

☐ ass res pe

⑤ GET

⑥ RESOURCES
☐ people's /skills
☐ techology
☐ food
☐ space
☐ materials

⑦ REALISATION of the project
getting done!
do the event

⑧ end EVALUA

⑨

N'T FORGET...
• SVALIZING /RECORDING everything
• FINE GOALS FOR EVERY MEETING
• KE BREAKS, HAVE ENERGIZERS :)
• HAVE IN PROCESS EVALUATION, REFLECTION ND CELEBRATE SMALL "VICTORIES"
• AVE A BEER (Robert made me write it down :D

Introduction to Knowmad Society

JOHN W. MORAVEC

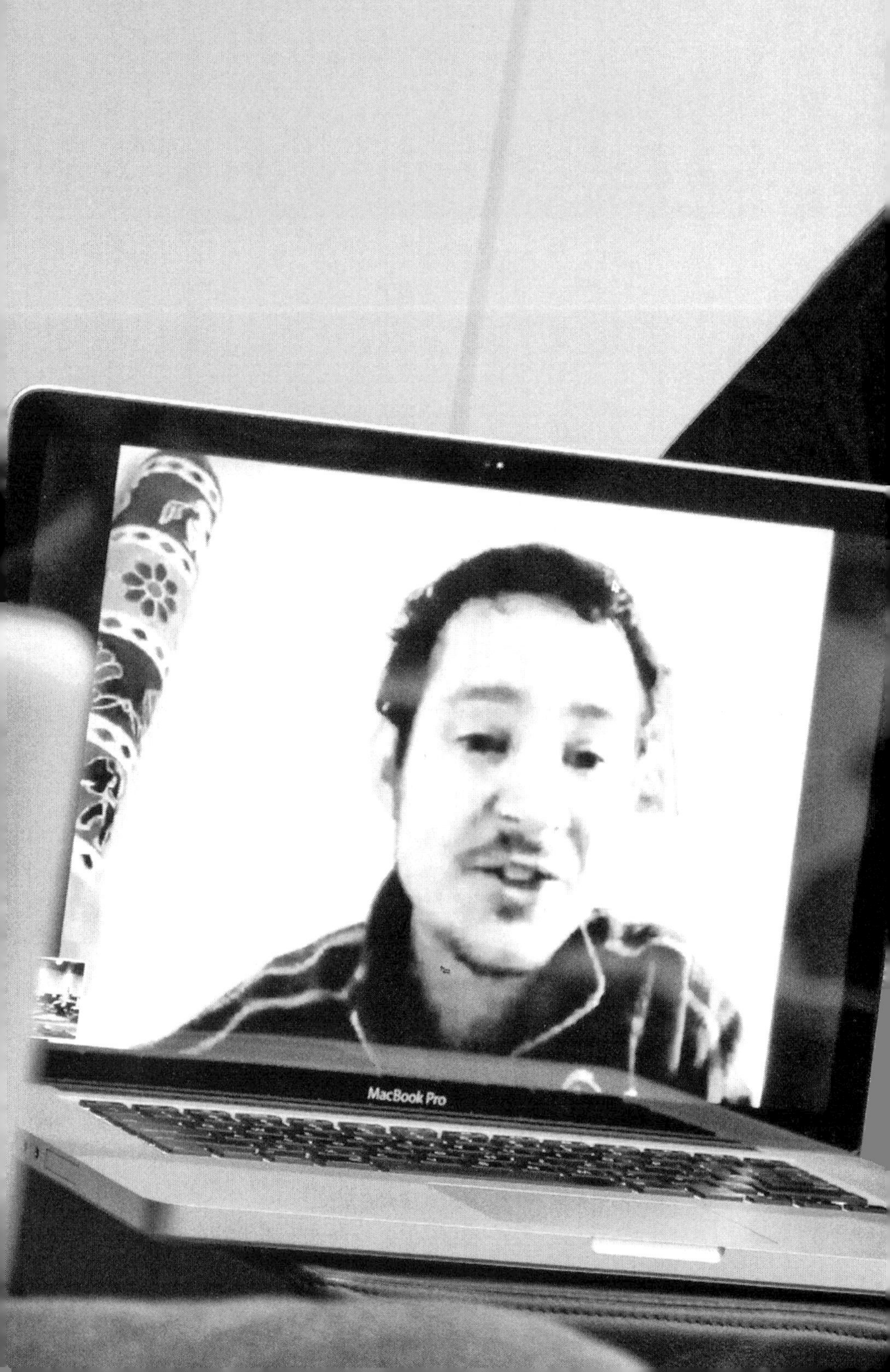
MacBook Pro

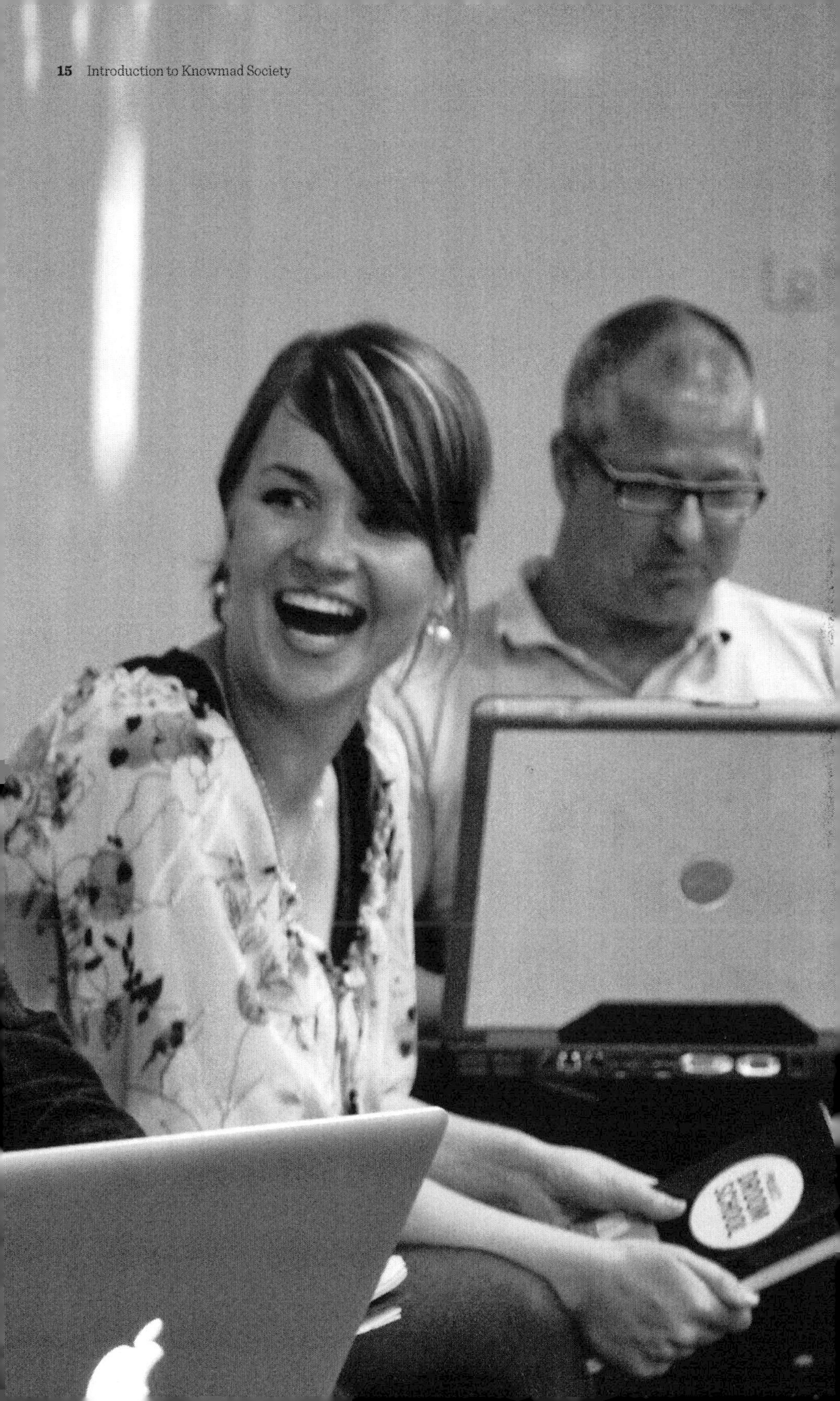

The emergence of *Knowmad Society* impacts everybody. It is a product of the changes in a world driven by exponential accelerating technological and social change, globalization, and a push for more creative and context-driven innovations. It is both exciting and frightening. It presents us with new opportunities, challenges, and responsibilities. And, we recognize that in a world of accelerating change, the future is uncertain. This prompts a key question: In a world consumed with uncertainty, how can we ensure the success of ourselves as individuals, our communities, and the planet?

This book explores the future of learning, work, and how we relate with each other in this emerging paradigm. In a blog post at *Education Futures*, I defined a *knowmad* as:

[...] a nomadic knowledge worker –that is, a creative, imaginative, and innovative person who can work with almost anybody, anytime, and anywhere. Industrial society is giving way to knowledge and innovation work. Whereas industrialization required people to settle in one place to perform a very specific role or function, the jobs associated with knowledge and information workers have become much less specific concerning task and place. Moreover, technologies allow for these new paradigm workers to work within broader options of space, including "real," virtual, or blended. Knowmads can instantly reconfigure and recontextualize their work environments, and greater mobility is creating new opportunities. (Moravec, 2008)

In other words, knowmads are extensions of Peter Drucker's (1992) *knowledge workers* concept, embracing the convergence of accelerating technological change and globalization. In particular, the use of advanced information and communications technologies enable knowmads to work beyond pre-19th century notions of nation states, corporate identity, and community identity. For some, knowmadism is realized through leveraging social media (i.e., Twitter or blogs) that add an additional layer of social and/or professional activities that defy the confinement to particular geographies and operational rules they may have been restricted to as recently as 10 years ago. For others, knowmads engage in work that is transnational, transcultural, and post-organizational in scope. And, a few select others may develop and apply such individual expertise that their work in new context creation enables them to be considered postnational and postcultural actors in their own right.

Knowmads are valued for the personal knowledge that they possess, and this knowledge gives them a competitive advantage. Knowmads are also responsible for designing their own futures. This represents a massive shift from agricultural, industrial, and information-based work in which our relationships and responsibilities were static and clearly defined by others.

IN THE PAST, WE APPLIED FOR JOBS. NOW WE ARE ASKED TO DESIGN OUR WORK.

By 2020, we project 45% of the Western workforce will be *knowmadic*. Moreover, this number will grow. That is, the jobs we take on and the ways in which we relate with each other will require less specificity about task and place. Knowmads can instantly reconfigure and recontextualize their work environments, and advances in mobility afforded by technological development leads to the continuous creation of new opportunities. A knowmad is only employed on a job as long as he or she can add value to an organization. If not, it's time to move on to the next gig.

Knowmads differentiate their jobs from work. *Jobs* are positions, gigs, or other forms of employment. *Work* is longer term in scope, and relates to the creation of meaningful outcomes. One's work differs from a career in Knowmad Society. Whereas a career is something that "carries" a person throughout life, an individual's work is a collection of activities that are backed with elements that are purposive at the personal level. In other words, the results of a knowmad's work are that person's responsibility alone.

Knowmads strive to continually define and refine their work. This can be expressed through occupying various jobs, apprenticeships, entrepreneurship, social activities, etc. If the knowmad once made a difference at their job, but there is little new opportunity for creating change, then it's time to move on. Without having a purposive direction to herd one's various jobs into work, we must question if that person has found his or her way.

Knowmad Society brings in a futures orientation, projecting not only the future of our workforce, but also examines the social, educational, and political implications for developing human capital that is relevant for the 21st century. We are at a crossroads where we can design a new human renaissance, built on leveraging our imagination, creativity and innovation – or we can doom ourselves to repeating the mistakes of our past.

This book builds on the ideas of many others who also observe the rise of Knowmad Society. Intriguing examples include:

- At the 2011 Lift Conference, Yasmine Abbas shared her vision of **neo-nomadism**, which she constructed from an urban planning perspective. Mobility is increasing, spatially, mentally, and electronically. This, in turn, creates new opportunities and challenges for how we integrate interpersonally and as organized cities (see Abbas, 2011).
- **Digital nomads**, as defined in Wikipedia ("Digital nomad," n.d.), are: "individuals that leverage digital technologies to perform their work duties, and more generally conduct their lifestyle in a nomadic manner. Such workers typically work remotely—from home, coffee shops and public libraries to collaborate with teams across the globe." This is an idea that Makimoto and Manners (1997) explored extensively in their book, *Digital nomad*.
- **1099 workers** – independent contractors (named from their frequent use of the U.S. Internal Revenue Service form 1099) – are a growing segment of the economy in the United States (see esp. Kotkin, 2012).
- Richard Florida developed the concept of the **creative class** of innovation and context-creation workers, consisting of a super-creative core, traditional knowledge workers, and new Bohemians (Florida, 2004; Florida, 2005).

- Richard Oliver (2007) discusses **purposive drift** – a need to connect with our inner humanness as we explore uncertain futures. Even if we are not sure where we our lives are going, as individuals, we need to develop a sense of purpose, or we would be simply lost.
- The U.S. Air Force, in its futures-based research, warns of hyper-powered individuals, aided by technologies, that may create more harm and havoc than any nation could in the previous century. The technological elimination of time and distance barriers means a greater number of individuals and organizations will play a role in charting future societies (Geis et al., p. xv).

...and so on.

The bottom line: Individual talent is becoming increasingly important in the 21st century. What one knows and can do with their knowledge in differing contextual formats drives their employability. In other words, people who can innovate and generate new value with their knowledge will lead employment growth. Those who do not will be replaced by machines, outsourced, or be outmoded by those who can (inspired by Clarke, 1980, p. 96).

In 2010, **Cristóbal Cobo** and I started the *Invisible learning* project, which was intended to result in Spanish and English-language editions of a book freely available under a Creative Commons license. We got sidetracked when the University of Barcelona Press contacted us, and indicated that they would like to publish it – but in Spanish only (as "Aprendizaje Invisible"). They were great to work with, and allowed us to release a free digital edition of the book in 2011. The product was a hit and over 50,000 copies were distributed in the first year (that we could count) – not bad for an education text!

The chapters Cobo and I share in this book are the direct descendants from the *Invisible learning* project. In the first chapter, I introduce the Knowmad Society concept in the context of redesigning education. This is a translation and update of Chapter 1 in *Invisible learning*, where I describe the transitions from what I label *Society 1.0* through *Society 3.0*. In the following chapter, Cobo provides a summary of key points we made elsewhere in the book, with updates, and more meaningful contextualization for Knowmad Society. While I focus on theory construction, Cobo connects it with policy studies and perspectives.

The impact of the remixing of places and social relationships on education cannot be ignored any longer. Students in Knowmad Society should learn, work, play, and share in almost any configuration. Nevertheless, there is little evidence to support any claim that education systems are moving toward a knowmad-enabled paradigm. We need to ask ourselves: *What are we educating for?* Are we educating to create factory workers and bureaucrats? Or, are we educating to create innovators, capable of leveraging their imagination and creativity?

Thieu Besselink offers an aesthetic approach toward re-imagining teaching in Knowmad Society, where teachers need to refocus from information delivery and measurements toward one where, together with students, they aim to build something new and meaningful for everybody. Rather than worrying about learning in top-down approaches to education, he offers a pathway for reinventing teachers as *learning choreographers* –guides who, "tease out experiences, sources of inspiration, and energy that can be the building blocks for the Quest."

Christel Hartkamp offers a different approach than the policy-driven schemes Cobo suggests, and argues that for youth to become successful in Knowmad Society, they must be enabled to find and build their own way, which requires skill development that is not present in mainstream education. Reflecting on her own experiences, she presents a case for expanding Sudbury-type education to best enable children to, "grow up as self-starters, showing initiative and entrepreneurialism, knowing how to use knowledge, their talents, and how to make decisions on the basis of their own judgments."

Pieter Spinder co-founded the Knowmads Business School in Amsterdam in 2009. The school offers an alternative platform for youth interested in developing their creative entrepreneurial skills in sustainable, socially innovative contexts. He jokes that students do not earn a diploma, but they have the possibility of earning a tattoo when they finish. But, like tattooing one's self, the school provides for the possibility for personal design and (re)definition – this individual-level development and expression is critical for success in Knowmad Society.

Edwin de Bree and **Bianca Stokman** relate their experiences in flattening hierarchical organizations. That is, in Knowmad Society, they ask if we need many layers of management, or can we form organizational structures that empower people to serve as their own "bosses" and do what is right for the institution? They provide several examples from their own work in "de-hierarching" organizations, and discuss the potentials for not only cost savings, but also for new opportunities provided by an empowered workforce.

Christine Renaud runs a Canadian startup called E-180. Utilizing social technologies, they are working to take learning out of classrooms and other formal environments, and instead embedding it into places that are more natural for humans – namely coffee shops. She reflects on the knowledge-sharing meetings that her company facilitates, and argues there is a hunger for collaborative learning that we can embed into society. Education researchers have been talking a lot about life-long learning, but what about life-long *teaching*?

Ronald van den Hoff has built a business out of supporting knowmads. I was pleased to meet him in 2009 after we realized that we were both working with nearly identical "Society 3.0" models (he prefers to label his "Society30" to match the URL of his recent book, Society 3.0: www.society30.com). His company, Seats2Meet.com, provides not only co-working spaces for knowmadic workers, but also blends in technologies that help enable collaboration, co-creation, and building productive relationships with others. In his contribution to this volume, he argues that knowmads are an essential component of "Organization 3.0" – and engaging them in the co-construction of his business has been very rewarding.

Finally, **U.S. Sen. Gary Hart** presents an insightful afterword that calls for policy leaders to wake up to the realities of Knowmad Society, and attend to its support as a matter of maintaining security among nations. Knowmads break down barriers rather than create new ones, and we must define new public responsibilities to provide for positive futures for citizens, nations, and our planet.

We provide a diverse range of perspectives, but unite under the core notions that the future is becoming much more unpredictable and old social structures have less value – especially those connected with education. Above all, we agree that we can lead with change today.

There is a strong Dutch presence in this book, and it is by no coincidence that the Dutch are breaking the path in realizing Knowmad Society. They have had a head start, aided by the geography of the *Randstad* conurbation, which connects many smaller cities together in a larger metropolitan-like area. Central to its success is a reliable rail network. Traveling by train to various cities to work and meet with others has become an activity as casual as taking the subway to a regular work place in a regular, concentrated city. In essence, many Dutch citizens are already nomadic in where they work – and growing into this mode of work is a natural transition.

Change is naturally frightening for humans, and living in Knowmad Society implies that the "securities" that we enjoyed in the past are obsolete (e.g., life-long employment at an organization, the promise of retirement, and steady streams of income). Indeed there are many challenges, and they can be construed as opportunities for knowmadic workers and policy makers to co-create new solutions. We instead choose to focus on the positive features of Knowmad Society – and how to generate positive outcomes.

In our approach, we differentiate little between learning and working. Knowmadic thinking and individual-level entrepreneurship exposes the fuzzy metaspaces in between each, opening new opportunities for new blends of formal, informal, non-formal and serendipitous learning. As in the *Invisible learning project*, we focus on educating for personal knowledge creation that cannot be measured easily. In the business world, this is reflected in flattening our organizational relationships ("de-hierarchizing") and *attending to* the inherent chaos and ambiguity in knowmadic systems, rather than fighting it (inspired esp. by Allee, 2003 & McElroy, 2003).

I organized this book to present a spectrum of ideas from the abstract and academic to the practical. My editing philosophy is not to conform each author's chapter to a unitary perspective, but rather to present an ecology of perspectives – in their own words. When reading this volume, you will read many incongruities and outright contradictions. They are all intended. Nobody knows the future, and we do not pretend to have all of the correct answers. What we hope, however, is that we will provoke you to join the dialogue.

PLEASE BREAK THE RULES. WE DID.

This book embodies a conversation in process. It is meant to be rough on the edges. We present our ideas as sparks to ignite dialogue, and invite your input and further development. My philosophical approach to assembling this book is to present the ideas of each author as his or her own. In my editing, this meant that I touched the text of each as little as I could so that individual voices and opinions can best emerge. And, we want to hear your voice, too.

If you are holding onto a paper copy of this book, please do not treat it like a book. Write on it, draw on the margins, highlight the parts you like, and write "bullshit" over the parts you do not like. Tear out pages; mix in your own ideas, and share alike with others. This entire volume is Creative Commons licensed, which means that we encourage you to copy, redistribute, and remix this work. All that we ask is that you share it alike with others, give proper credit for the ideas you use, and let us know how you have added to the conversation.

On behalf of the team that contributed to this book, we look forward to co-developing Knowmad Society with you.

REFERENCES

Abbas, Y. (2011). Design for transience: Distributed selves/distributed spaces. Retrieved from klewel.com/conferences/lift11/index.php?talkID=11

Allee, V. (2003). *The future of knowledge: Increasing prosperity through value networks*. Amsterdam; Boston: Butterworth-Heinemann.

Clarke, A. C. (1980). Electronic tutors. *OMNI, 2*(9), 76–78:96. Retrieved from https://ia701206.us.archive.org/29/items/omni-magazine-1980-06/OMNI_1980_06.pdf

Cobo, C., & Moravec, J. W. (2011). *Aprendizaje invisible: Hacia una nueva ecología de la educación*. Barcelona: Laboratori de Mitjans Interactius / Publicacions i Edicions de la Universitat de Barcelona.

Digital nomad. (n.d.). In *Wikipedia*. Retrieved August 26, 2012, from en.wikipedia.org/wiki/Digital_nomad

Florida, R. L. (2004). *The rise of the creative class: And how it's transforming work, leisure, community and everyday life*. New York, NY: Basic Books.

Florida, R. L. (2005). *The flight of the creative class: The new global competition for talent* (1st ed.). New York: HarperBusiness.

Geis, J. P., Kinnan, C. J., Hailes, T., Foster, H. A., & Blanks, D. (2009). *Blue Horizons II: Future capabilities and technologies for the Air Force in 2030.* Maxwell Airforce Base, Alabama: Air Force Press. Retrieved from www.au.af.mil/au/awc/awcgate/cst/csat65.pdf

Kotkin, J. (2012). The rise of the 1099 economy: More Americans are becoming their own bosses. *Forbes.* Retrieved from www.forbes.com/sites/joelkotkin/2012/07/25/the-rise-of-the-1099-economy-more-americans-are-becoming-their-own-bosses/

Makimoto, T., & Manners, D. (1997). *Digital nomad.* New York: Wiley.

McElroy, M. W. (2003). *The new knowledge management: Complexity, learning, and sustainable innovation.* Burlington, MA: Butterworth-Heinemann.

Moravec, J. W. (2008, November 20). Knowmads in Society 3.0. Retrieved from www.educationfutures.com/2008/11/20/knowmads-in-society-30/

Oliver, R. (2007). Purposive drift: Making it up as we go along. Retrieved from changethis.com/manifesto/31.06.PurposiveDrift/pdf/31.06.PurposiveDrift.pdf

notes

Notes

notes

notes

Rethinking human capital development in Knowmad Society

JOHN W. MORAVEC

'We need to train kids how to think, not what to think.'

'NEW TECHNOLOGIES SHOULD NOT BE USED TO DO THE SAME OLD STUFF.'

'Educational reform is not worth fighting for. We need a revolution.'

'KNOWMADS ARE CREATIVE, IMAGINATIVE, AND INNOVATIVE PEOPLE WHO CAN WORK WITH ALMOST ANYBODY, ANYTIME, AND ANYWHERE.'

JOHN W. MORAVEC

'1.0 SCHOOLS CANNOT TEACH 3.0 KIDS'

'WE NEED TO CREATE NEW, PURPOSIVE USES FOR TECHNOLOGIES TO ENABLE US TO DO THINGS IN EDUCATION THAT WE COULD NOT DREAM OF BEFORE.'

SUMMARY

**RETHINKING HUMAN CAPITAL
DEVELOPMENT IN KNOWMAD SOCIETY**
~ John W. Moravec ~

A *knowmad* is a nomadic knowledge and innovation worker – that is, a creative, imaginative, and innovative person who can work with almost anybody, anytime, and anywhere (Moravec, 2008a). Knowmads are valued for the personal knowledge that they possess and for the purposive application of their knowledge in different contexts (i.e., jobs).

This chapter presents a framework for conceptualizing changes in society, driven by the forces of globalization, an expanding knowledge society, and accelerating change – and places the framework within the context of a society in transition from an industrial paradigm to one that is driven by applied personal knowledge capital.

In our education systems, Knowmad Society necessitates the transformation from industrial-era, "banking" pedagogies (see esp. Freire, 1968) that transmit "just in case" information and knowledge toward modes that utilize invisible spaces of learning to develop personally- and socially-meaningful, actionable knowledge.

As organizations, communities, and nations, we need to set visions for the futures we will co-create, and act upon them. Given rates of accelerating technological, social and economic change, we cannot wait. The revolution in learning and human capital development needs to begin now. This may mean starting out small, working in parallel with entrenched systems, but it also means that we need to lead by example.

I present a framework for conceptualizing changes in society, driven by the forces of globalization, an expanding knowledge society, and accelerating change. The framework is centered on three social paradigms, which I label 'Society 1.0,' 'Society 2.0,' and 'Society 3.0' (Moravec, 2008c) – expressed as Industrial Society, Knowledge Society, and Knowmad Society.

Society 1.0 reflects the norms and practices of pre-industrial to industrial civilization. *Society 2.0* refers to the radical social transformations that we are experiencing today, largely due to technological change. The *3.0* or *Knowmad Society* points to a state of society that is developing into our near future, where accelerating technological change is projected to have huge transformative implications. This chapter also considers the human capital development consequences and necessary transformations in education to meet the needs of a rapidly transforming society, and looks into some of the challenges facing Knowmad Society in an era of accelerating change.

Note: This chapter is adapted from Moravec, J. W. (2011). Desde la sociedad 1.0 a la sociedad 3.0. In C. Cobo & J. W. Moravec (Eds.), *Aprendizaje invisible: Hacia una nueva ecología de la educación* (pp. 47-74). Barcelona: Laboratori de Mitjans Interactius / Publicacions i Edicions de la Universitat de Barcelona. (Under Creative Commons license.)

The paradoxical co-existence of 'Education 1.0' in 'Society 3.0'

Society 1.0

Society 1.0 refers to the agricultural to industrial-based society that was largely present throughout the 18th century through the end of the 20th century. In the early portion of this period, economic activity was centered on family-based enterprises. Children learned at home, and children worked at home. Kids and adults were engaged cross-generationally. Not only were children valuable contributors to the economy at all levels, but adults and kids learned from each other. This paradigm facilitated "learning by doing," which was formally adopted by organizations such as 4-H, and embraced the principle that if we teach youth ideas and skills, they would, in turn, teach their parents (4-H, n.d.).

The rise of the industrial economy saw growth in wage and salary-based enterprises. Kids began to work at low-level and often dangerous jobs until they were segregated from the workplace to protect their welfare. This also signaled the industrialization of education, where, separated from the primary production economy, children were placed into an institutional mechanism of compulsory schooling where kids learned skills from adults (and not vice-versa), and eventually emerged from the system as "educated," young adults, immediately employable for the industrial economy.

In Society 1.0, we interpreted data in an industrial manner – leading to the information age. By and large, our relationships were hierarchical. That is, it was easy to tell how we related with each other. Companies had reporting structures that were easy to decipher. And, we had siloed jobs and roles within organizations and communities. We did everything we could to avoid chaos and ambiguity. Leading toward the end of the 20th century, this model worked fine. It was easy to understand. It was easy to operationalize. Moreover, it benefited from an education system that produced workers for the industrial-modeled economy.

By the end of the 20th century, the industrialization of education and proliferation of meritocratic academic structures in the 1.0 paradigm all but eliminated the recognition of "learning by doing." This evolved norm *generally* provided socioeconomic advantages for those that successfully navigated the industrialized meritocracy (better jobs, better pay) than those who avoided it or did not survive the system.

Society 2.0

The appearance of Society 2.0 is associated with the emergence of the knowledge society that materialized in the 20th century (see esp. Drucker, 1969, 1985). To become meaningful, information needed to be interpreted, necessitating the creation of knowledge workers. However, as Polyani (1968) explains, the nature of knowledge, itself, is *personal* and is composed of tacit and explicit components. Explicit knowledge is easy to transfer from person to person, and can be communicated, for example, through books. Tacit knowledge, like knowing how to play the violin, is difficult to transfer, and is best developed by "learning by doing." These two forms of knowledge combine in the creation of *personally-constructed meanings* that defy the absolute objectivity of Society 1.0's industrial information model. Additionally, as social animals, humans engage in community activities and share their personal knowledge across ever-complex, networked systems. This growing ecosystem of personally-constructed meanings and values facilitated the creation of the field of *knowledge management* in the latter half of the 20th century, which attempted to manage the new elements of chaos and ambiguity related to personal knowledge that were inputted into organizational systems.

Advances in information and communications technologies (ICTs) facilitated the broadened production of socially-constructed meanings. Many of these advancements are made possible through the convergence of the Internet (which has become the symbol for all things networking – personal and technological) and globalization, opening potentials for globally-aware and globally-present social networks. Tools that harness ICTs are not only used to share ideas, but also to create new interpretations of the "reality" we live in. A few scholars (see, for example, Mahiri, 2004) recognize this as a "cut-and-paste" culture. One potent example of this cultural shift is hip-hop, which remixes and reuses sounds, lyrics, and imagery to create new meanings that are as much unique and individual to the hip-hop artist as the creator and the works' original sources. Other examples include the products of "Web 2.0" tools (see esp. Cobo Romaní & Pardo Kuklinski, 2007, for a detailed discussion) that allow individuals to harness new social networks to remix and share ideas and media (e.g., blogs, wikis, and YouTube).

The mass availability of these tools also allows everyday people to participate in an expanded array of vocations and citizen engagement. For example, tools such as blogs, Twitter and YouTube allow for the formation of citizen journalists, who are able to compete directly with mainstream media at a nearly negligible fraction of the cost that mainstream media needs to develop and deliver content. The technologies also allow for the formation of citizen scientists. By donating computing processing time, non-scientifically trained individuals can search for signs of extraterrestrial intelligence (*SETI@Home* project), search for a cure for cancer (*Folding@Home*), and examine stellar particles retrieved from space (*Stardust@Home*). Likewise, the Audubon Society has long relied on its social network of professional and amateur birdwatchers to generate a statistically accurate estimate of birds within a given area. Furthermore, technologies allow for the greater democratization of markets, creating citizen capitalists that invest and compete in a global market for ideas, talent, products, and other capital.

Socially-oriented ICTs carry constraints and limitations that force individuals to transform how they think and act. For example, Twitter limits message sizes to 140 characters or less, forcing content producers to deliver clear, concise messages in limited space.

These transformations are leading to new questions for social and educational theorists that are still being debated – and research suggests that these changes are impacting the fundamental organization of the human brain (see esp. Small & Vorgan, 2008). Some key questions arising are: Does Society 2.0 dumb people down, or are we creating a new, hyper-connected, social super-intelligence? If tech-savvy youth are composing their thoughts in 140 characters or less, are we facing a loss of literacy? In a world with Twitter, do we have any cognitive capacity to read full-length novels? In a world with YouTube, can we sit through feature length films? Is technological change, paired with globalization, leading to a loss of our cultural heritages? Finally, how can education remain relevant in a cut-and-paste society where information flows freely?

Society 3.0: Knowmad Society

> *"The future is already here – it's just not evenly distributed."*
> *–William Gibson (interviewed in Gladstone, 1999)*

For most of us, Society 3.0 is in the future – possibly in the distant future. But, for a few people leading the change toward this *proto-paradigm*, it is very real. Three drivers are leading us to the formation of the 3.0, knowmadic paradigm, which describes a world that is somewhere between "just around the corner" and "just beyond the horizon" of today's state-of-the-art:

1 Accelerating technological and social change;
2 Continuing globalization and horizontalization of knowledge and relationships (de-hierarchization); and,
3 Innovation society fueled by *knowmads*.

Kurzweil (1999) postulates a theory he labels the *Law of Accelerating Returns* to describe the evolutionary process that leads to accelerating technological and social change:

> As order exponentially increases, time exponentially speeds up (that is, the time interval between salient events grows shorter as time passes). (Kurzweil, 1999, p. 30)

Figure 1. Accelerating technological change

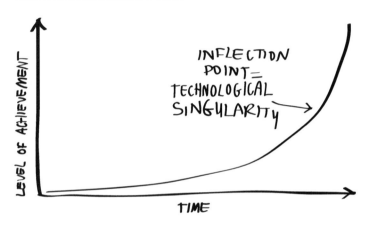

Note: The J-curve of accelerating change illustrates the exponential development and exponentially reduced costs of technologies. One example is evident in the evolution of microprocessors, which follow Moore's (1965) Law of doubling the number of transistors on integrated circuits every two years, while also reducing the costs of associated processing speed, memory capacities, etc. The inflection point on the graph is the approximate location of the Technological Singularity, at which point change occurs so rapidly that the human mind cannot imagine what will happen next. If this trend continues, and Moore's Law is followed for the next 600 years, a single microprocessor would have the computational equivalency of the known Universe (Krauss & Starkman, 2004).

In other words, change is occurring rapidly, and the pace of change is increasing at a rate that will defy human imagination. Kurzweil's idea is founded on the premise that as technologies evolve, technologies improve, costs decrease; and, in turn, the process of technological evolution advances and speeds itself up, creating a J-curve of exponential, accelerating change (see Figure 1, above). As technologies evolve, they will also prompt social transformations (Morgan, 1877).

This acceleration of change, however, is predicted to have an enormous impact on human imagination and our abilities to predict the future. Vinge (1993) terms the theoretical limit of human foresight and imagination (illustrated as the inflection point on the above graphic) as the *Technological Singularity*. As the rate of technological advancement increases, it will become more difficult for a human observer to predict or understand future technological advancements.

Given the rate of exponential advancement illustrated by Kurzweil (2005), the pace of technological advancements in the future may seem nearly simultaneous to human observers. Kurzweil further believes the Singularity will emerge as the complex, seemingly chaotic outcome of converging technologies (esp. genetics, nanotechnology, robotics, and the integration of these technologies with humans). Vinge (in Moravec, 2012) believes the best option for humanity is to merge with our technologies and build a "digital Gaia" of global human-technology integration and knowledge sharing. This merging with technologies could involve augmenting our bodies, engineering "improved" humans, and active involvement in the design of our successor species.

As noted previously, technological change facilitates social change. Near future technological advancements are therefore expected to ignite social transformations that defy human imagination today. Critics of the Technological Singularity, including Rushkoff (2013), contend that it is impossible to disentangle humans from technologies. It is not worthwhile to focus our attention on dealing with future change, as many of these transformations are already occurring today, and we need to become aware with their relationships with the present –and ourselves.

Predictably, the impacts of accelerating technological and social changes on education are enormous. Today's stakeholders in our youths' future must prepare kids for futures that none of us can even dream are possible.

Continuing globalization is leading to a horizontalized diffusion of knowledge in domains that were previously siloed, creating heterarchical relationships, and providing new opportunities for knowledge to be applied contextually in innovative applications. In the realm of teaching and learning, this means that we are becoming not only co-learners, but also co-teachers as we *co-constructively* produce new knowledge and new applications for our knowledge.

Table 1 summarizes key differences between the three social paradigms that we explore in this book. In the shift from Society 1.0 to Society 3.0, our basic relationships transform from linear, mechanistic, and deterministic connections to a new order that is highly non-linear, synergetic, and design-oriented. The effects of accelerating change suggest that causality, itself, may seem to express anticausal characteristics, due to the near instantaneousness of events experienced by a society in a period of continuous, accelerating change. Therefore, how reality is contextualized (and contextually responded to) becomes much more important to citizens in Society 3.0 than it was in previous paradigms.

Table 1. Societies 1.0 through 3.0 across various domains (inspired by Schwartz & Ogilvy, 1979)

Domain	1.0	2.0	3.0
Fundamental relationships	Simple	Complex	Complex creative (teleological)
Conceptualization of order	Hierarchic	Heterarchic	Intentional (self-organizing)
Relationship of parts	Mechanical	Holographic	Synergetic
Worldview	Deterministic	Indeterminate	Design
Causality	Linear	Mutual	Anticausal
Change Process	Assembly	Morphegenic	Creative destruction
Reality	Objective	Perspectival	Contextual
Place	Local	Globalizing	Globalized

Knowmads in Society 3.0

A *knowmad* is what I term a nomadic knowledge and innovation worker – that is, a creative, imaginative, and innovative person who can work with almost anybody, anytime, and anywhere (Moravec, 2008a). Knowmads are valued for the personal knowledge that they possess, and this knowledge gives them a competitive advantage in social and work contexts. Industrial society is giving way to knowledge and innovation work. Whereas the industrialization of Society 1.0 required people to settle in one place to perform a very specific role or function, the jobs associated with knowledge and information workers have become much less specific in regard to task and place. Moreover, technologies allow for these new paradigm workers to work either at a specific place, virtually, or in any blended combination. Knowmads can instantly reconfigure and recontextualize their work environments and relationships. Greater mobility afforded by technologies creates these new opportunities.

The remixing of people and ideas through digital and social formats has already become commonplace. Consider, for example, coffee shops. These environments have become the workplace of choice for many knowmads. What happens when an investment banker sits next to an architect and strikes up a conversation? What new ideas, products, and services might be created?

Knowmads:

1   Are not restricted to a specific age;
2   Build their personal knowledge through explicit information gathering and tacit experiences, and leverage their personal knowledge to produce new ideas;
3   Are able to contextually apply their ideas and expertise in various social and organizational configurations;
4   Are highly motivated to collaborate, and are natural networkers, navigating new organizations, cultures, and societies;
5   Use new technologies *purposively* to help them solve problems and transcend geographical limitations;
6   Are open to sharing what they know, and invite and support open access to information, knowledge, and expertise from others;
7   Can unlearn as quickly as they learn, adopting new ideas and practices as necessary;
8   Thrive in non-hierarchical networks and organizations;
9   Develop habits of mind and practice to learn continuously; and,
10 Are not afraid of failure.

Note: List inspired by Cobo (2008).

The remixing of places and social relationships implies that a tremendous impact on education is developing as well. Students in Knowmad Society should learn, work, play, and share in almost any configuration. But, there is little evidence to support any claim that formal education is moving toward the 3.0 paradigm.

When we compare the list of skills required of knowmads to the goals and outcomes of mainstream education, we must ask: Precisely *what* are we educating for? Are we educating to create factory workers and bureaucrats? Or, are we educating to create innovators, capable of leveraging their own imagination and creativity?

Legacy education: Factory of the state

The industrialization of Europe was accompanied by social, economic, and political transformations that impacted education directly. Regents sought to replace aristocratic rulers with citizens instilled with national pride and a willingness to work for the "good" of their country. At the same time, economic growth required more factory workers and government bureaucrats to manage the system as industrial society emerged.

To meet these needs, Frederick II of Prussia, initiated in 1763 what may be considered the most radical reform in the history of education: compulsory schooling. All children in Prussia between the ages of five and 13 were required to attend schools, which were developed into apparatuses of the state. Principles of industrial production were applied to classrooms, which were segregated by age. Pupils were aligned at desks, facing the head, where the teacher, bestowed with the absolute authority of the state, "downloaded" information and state ideology into the heads of students as if they were empty vessels.

The result: the state produced students that were loyal to the nation and had the potential of becoming capable factory workers and bureaucrats. This industrial model of compulsory education gained popularity in Europe, and, eventually, it was adopted throughout Western Civilization, where it remains the prevalent model of education today.

Important stuff!

Invisible learning: A new expression of human capital development in Knowmad Society

In the *Invisible learning* project, Cristóbal Cobo and I explored a panorama of options for the future development of education that are relevant today (see Cobo & Moravec, 2011). In our work, we did not propose a formal theory, but rather established a metatheory capable of integrating different ideas and perspectives. We describe this as a *proto-paradigm*, aligned with our visions of a knowmad-centric Society 3.0, which is still in the *beta* stage of construction.

Knowmad Society calls for the transformation from industrial-era, "banking" pedagogies (see esp. Freire, 1968) that transmit "just in case" information and knowledge (i.e., memorization of the world's capitals) toward modes that utilize the invisible spaces to develop personally- and socially- meaningful, actionable knowledge. There is growing recognition that people with unique, key knowledge and skills (i.e., knowmads) are critical for the success of modern organizations. Godin (2010) argues successful people in today's organizations serve as "linchpins." From an interview with Godin by Hyatt (2010), Godin states:

> *The linchpin insists on making a difference, on leading, on connecting with others and doing something I call art. The linchpin is the indispensable one, the one the company can't live without. This is about humanity, not compliance. (Hyatt, 2010)*

In their book, *The element*, Robinson & Aronica (2009) interview many people who have experienced extraordinary success in their careers, and identified that the people they spoke with found their "element" – that is, their success was largely due to the fact that they did something they enjoyed in addition to being good at it. This runs contrary to the "just in case" industrial model of education, and suggests that if we enable more people to pursue their passions and support them, we open possibilities for them to achieve meaningful success.

In the invisible learning proto-paradigm, the inherent chaos and ambiguity related to tremendous technological and social changes call for a resurgence of "learning by doing." In a sense, we are creating the future as we go along, and without a master plan to follow. As co-learners and co-teachers, we are co-responsible for helping each other find our own elements along our pathways of personal, knowmadic development.

How do we measure learning in the invisible spaces?

The cult of educational measurement

A key concern for policymakers and other stakeholders in education is, *what is being learned?* In an education system focused on industrial information delivery, this is an important quality control issue. People responsible for aligning resources for learning, need to know what works and what does not.

The linearity of the industrial paradigm thrives on mechanical processes. For example, groups of learners are expected to read books progressively, chapter-by-chapter, and recite the information and "facts" they acquired linearly through memorization. In this paradigm, the use of summative evaluation (i.e., tests) is *de rigueur*. And, this is very convenient for governments. It suggests that the knowledge of students can be represented, tabulated, and communicated as numbers in a spreadsheet report.

Throughout the world, we have adopted this culture of industrial learning and evaluation *en masse*, and created a cult of educational measurement to support it. In the United States, this is manifested through the testing requirements of the No Child Left Behind Act. In Spain, the cult is evident in the filtering processes that lead to the Prueba de Acceso. In the United Kingdom, it is expressed within the National Curriculum (Education Reform Act of 1988). And so on.

This industrial model serves the needs of government overseers, but does little to meet the development needs of individual learners. With policies with names like "No Child Left Behind," it is hard to disagree: *is the alternative to leave children behind?* The unfortunate reality, however, is that, in these industrial-modeled policies, we tend to leave many children behind. These testing-centric regimes produce exactly the wrong labor products for the 21st century, but they are appropriate for what the world needed from the 19th century through World War II. As Robinson (2001) and others have argued, these fractured memorization models oppose the creative, synthetical thinking required for work in the new economy and effective citizenship.

Leapfrogging beyond the cult of educational measurement
When we focus on how to learn, not what to learn, learning becomes invisible.

In the knowmadic, 3.0 proto-paradigm, rote, "just in case" memorization needs to be replaced with learning that is intended to be personally meaningful for all participants in the learning experience. Moreover, the application of personal knowledge toward *innovative* problem solving takes primacy over the regurgitation of prior information memorized or "facts." In essence, students become *knowledge brokers* (Meyer, 2010).

Approaches that enable invisible learning also permit students to act on their knowledge, applying what they know to solve problems – including problems that have not been solved before. This contextual, purposive application of personal knowledge to create innovative solutions negates the value of standardized testing, which does not promote imaginative exploration, creative thinking, or innovative actions.

The "learning by doing" aspect of invisible learning that focuses on *how* to learn rather than *what* to learn suggests that measurement or evaluation activities need to be outcomes-based in the same way that we evaluate innovations:

- What happened?
- Did something new happen? (Was it something unexpected?)
- Was there a positive benefit?
- What can others learn from the experience?

Although there is a large body of literature supporting the need for formative assessments in education (see, for example, Armstrong, 1985; Marzano, 2003; Stiggins, 2008; Stiggins, Arter, Chappuis, & Chappuis, 2007), as well as a rich educational literature theory base that suggests we need to move toward learner-centered learning (perhaps the most vocal being Dewey, 1915; Freire, 2000), summative evaluations still persist in formal learning environments that present little value to the learner. Strategies to bring the informal into the formal are already present and widely adopted in business, industry, and, ironically, within some teacher education programs.

For example, Pekka Ihanainen (2010) explains that Finnish vocational teacher education is built on a dialogical professional development model. Knowledge and expertise areas of the teachers in training are identified and compared with their occupational competency requirements and goals. Following this assessment, career development trajectories and educational pathways are developed. The system is not only designed to determine how teachers in training meet government requirements, but also relates to their individual interests and professional development goals.

Releasing ourselves from the cult of measurement requires faith and confidence that we are always learning. As we observed in the *Invisible learning* project, as human beings, we are always engaged in learning – it is one of our most natural activities.

Implementing knowmadic learning: Making the invisible visible

The difficulties in mainstreaming invisible, knowmadic approaches to learning in Western education are daunting. Formal systems are deeply entrenched. Governments believe in a formal approach (it looks good on paper and within state and national budgets). Entire industries (i.e., textbooks, educational measurement) are built around it. And, the scale of the industrialization of education leaves many people wondering if it's worth fighting against. The education-industrial complex is massive.

The system is further reinforced, by design, to change at a glacial pace. While markets can transform and reinvent themselves virtually overnight, governments cannot. They are designed to be slow and deliberative. As a result, they tend to lag significantly, and react to change more often than they *proactively design* or *preact* to create beneficial changes.

Paradoxically, despite being key components of systems most responsible for developing human capital and human development futures, educational bodies are designed to change *even slower*. Educational institutions and systems report to governments, respond to governmental policies, and align their programs to satisfy requirements and funding formulae established by legislative bodies. Moreover, these criteria, including establishing *what* to teach, depends on who sits on what committee at any given time. By relying on personalities, political gamesmanship, and feedback-looped special interests from the education-industrial complex, many question if the system has perhaps become too large, too slow, and too blind to the realities of today.

The problem is, *the emerging pressures of Society 3.0 require educational transformation today*. Schools need to develop students that can design future jobs, industries, and knowledge fields that we have yet to dream of. Schools need to operate as generators of the future, not laggards.

Is educational reform worth fighting for?

No.

Rather, it is time to start anew. As Sir Ken Robinson eloquently states, we need a *revolution*, not reform (TED, 2010). Revolutions are difficult to ignite. An entire genre of literature that Carmen Tschofen terms "change manifestos" has emerged in education that is rich in calls for change, but falls flat on making change happen (Moravec, 2010). The system, perhaps, has too much inertia. As Harkins and I suggest in our "Leapfrog University" memo series to the University of Minnesota, a *parallel* approach may be necessary (Harkins & Moravec, 2006).

Rather than fighting the system, students, parents, communities, and other life-long learners can invest in establishing parallel, new schools and/or networks of learning, discovering, innovating, and sharing. And, some communities are already leading the way with innovative initiatives. For example:

- **Shibuya University Network** (Japan): "Yasuaki Sakyo, president of Shibuya University, believes that education should be life-long. At Shibuya, courses are free and open to all; classes take place in shops, cafes and outside; and anyone can be a teacher" (CNN, 2007). In essence, the entire community and its environment have become the co-learners, co-teachers, and classroom.
- **The Bank of Common Knowledge** (*Banco Común de Conocimientos*, Spain): "is a pilot experience dedicated to the research of social mechanisms for the collective production of contents (sic), mutual education, and citizen partici-pation. It is a laboratory platform where we explore new ways of enhancing the distribution channels for practical and informal knowledge, as well as how to share it" (Bank of Common Knowledge, n.d.).
- **TED.com** (*Technology, Entertainment, Design*, USA): challenges lecture-based education by creating "a clearinghouse that offers free knowledge and inspira-tion from the world's most inspired thinkers, and also a community of curious souls to engage with ideas and each other" (TED, n.d.).
- **Knowmads Business School** (Netherlands): an alternative "learning by doing" higher education experience, described later in this book, is not authorized by the government to issue diplomas, but invites students to earn a tattoo, if they like.

Redefining human capital development

To move forward in making invisible learning visible, we need to engage in conversations on what futures we want to create. We need to clarify our visions of where and who we want to be. In China, India, and throughout much of the developing world, the vision is simple: catch up to the West through planned development. However, in the United States, Europe, and much of the rest of the Western world, concrete visions of where we want to be in the future are absent. I assert that either we do not know where we want to be in the future, or we lack the foresight to imagine ourselves in a future that is very different from what we experience today.

The consequence is that we are not making investments to our human capital development systems that will enable us to meet needs set by future challenges. We need to prepare our youth and other members of society for a future and workforce we cannot yet imagine. Moreover, given the potential for today's children to be engaged productively in a "post-Singularity" era, it is important to assist them in the development of skills and habits of mind that will foster life-long learning and continuous, innovative applications of their personal knowledge.

The lack of vision –and preactive engagement on it– affects not only education, but also other areas of our socioeconomic well-being. Bob Herbert (2010) wrote for the New York Times on the United States' new unwillingness to invest in ideas that could increase potentials for future growth and prosperity:

> *The United States is not just losing its capacity to do great things. It's losing its soul. It's speeding down an increasingly rubble-strewn path to a region where being second rate is good enough. (Herbert, 2010)*

As organizations, communities, and nations, we need to set visions for the futures we will co-create, and act upon them. Throughout the remainder of this volume, we explore some of the methods individuals, teams, and organizations may employ to help develop our visions of the future.

Using technologies purposively

When engaged in conversations about invisible learning or other innovations in education, there is a tendency for people to gravitate their thoughts toward *technology* as if it can serve as a "silver bullet" to slay the metaphorical werewolf of the persistence of the industrial, Education 1.0 model. Innovation in education does not mean "technology." Douglas Adams (1999) elaborated on the challenges of defining the purpose of technologies:

> *Another problem with the net is that it's still 'technology', and 'technology', as the computer scientist Bran Ferren memorably defined it, is 'stuff that doesn't work yet.' We no longer think of chairs as technology, we just think of them as chairs. But there was a time when we hadn't worked out how many legs chairs should have, how tall they should be, and they would often 'crash' when we tried to use them. Before long, computers will be as trivial and plentiful as chairs (and a couple of decades or so after that, as sheets of paper or grains of sand) and we will cease to be aware of the things. In fact I'm sure we will look back on this last decade and wonder how we could ever have mistaken what we were doing with them for 'productivity.' (Adams, 1999)*

Moreover, we use the term "technology" to describe new tools that we do not understand. That is, the *purposive* uses of "technologies" are not well defined. As a result, in educational contexts, we often take the best technologies and squander the opportunities they afford us. Roger Schank (in Molist, 2010) puts it bluntly:

> *It's the same garbage, but placed differently. Schools select new technologies and ruin them. For example, when television came, every school put one in each classroom, but used it to do exactly the same things as before. The same with computers today. Oh, yes, we have e-learning! What does it mean? Then they give the same terrible course, but online, using computers in a stupid way. (Molist, 2010)*

Douglas Rushkoff adds a critique in an interview with Paul Zenke, where he suggests our obsessions with technologies obscure real social interaction and learning:

> *[...] as we spend more of our time fetishizing these devices these new avenues for education, I feel like the human bonds of the classroom, actual people who are in the same room together, that loses its cohesiveness, it loses its power. The big challenge for people today is doing very simple things like maintaining eye contact, generating rapport with other human beings. Understanding how to work with others – that's the kind of stuff you can get in a classroom, and you can't get on a Wii when you're at home. I'm really encouraging educators not to use classroom time to have kids all staring at the SMART Board or at their iPads, and instead to use that valuable few hours of class time you have helping kids and students orient to one another in real space. Because 94% of communication that happens non-verbally is starting to get lost as our noses get closer and closer into our smart phones. (Rushkoff in Zenke, 2013)*

With these critiques in mind, the invisible learning approach to technology is *purposive, pragmatic* and centered at *improving the human experience* at its core. Specifically, this means that it is:

1   **Well-defined:** The purpose and applications of particular technologies need to be specified. Bringing in technologies for the sake of using technologies will likely lead to their misuse, underuse, and/or the creation of unintended outcomes.

2   **Focused on developing *mindware*:** The focus of technologies should not be on hardware or software, but on how they enhance our minds – that is, the focus is placed on how technologies can support our imaginations, creativity, and help us innovate.

3   **Social:** The use of technologies is often a social experience, and their social applications should be addressed. This includes leveraging social media tools for learning such as Facebook, Twitter, etc., which are commonly blocked from formal school settings.

4   **Experimental:** Embraces the concept of "learning by doing," and allows for trial and error which can lead to successes and the occasional failure – but does not create failures.

5   **Continuously evolving:** As an area for "beta testing" new ideas and approaches to problems, it is continuously in a state of remixing and transformation. As society evolves continuously, so must our learning and sharing.

Who gets to leapfrog to Knowmad Society?

Complicating invisible learning is a problem of equity and equality. Is it appropriate for a select group of "invisible learners" to leapfrog ahead of peers who may be trapped within the paradigm of Education 1.0? If 1% of the population benefits from invisible learning approaches relevant for Knowmad Society, what should we do about the other 99%? Should they not have the right to leapfrog ahead, too?

I believe so. However, I also recognize the incredible inertia mainstream Education 1.0 possesses. Given the rates of accelerating technological, social, and economic change, we cannot wait. The revolution in learning and human capital development needs to begin now. This may mean starting out small, and working in parallel with entrenched systems. But, it also means that we need to lead by example to build a workforce ready for Knowmad Society today.

REFERENCES

4-H. (n.d.). 4-H history. Retrieved October 4, 2010, from www.4-h.org/about/4-h-history/

Adams, D. N. (1999). How to stop worrying and learn to love the Internet. Retrieved October 10, 2010, from www.douglasadams.com/dna/19990901-00-a.html

Armstrong, J. S. (1985). *Long range forecasting: From crystal ball to computer* (2nd ed.). New York: Wiley.

Bank of Common Knowledge. (n.d.). About the Bank of Common Knowledge (BCK). Retrieved October 5, 2010, from www.bancocomun.org/Wiki/queEsBcc/

CNN. (2007). Interview: Yasuaki Sakyo. Retrieved October 5, 2010, from edition.cnn.com/2007/TECH/11/01/sakyo.qa/

Cobo, C. (2008, April 22). Skills for a Knowledge/Mind Worker Passport (19 commandments). *Education Futures.* Retrieved from www.educationfutures.com/2008/04/22/skills-for-a-knowledgemind-worker-passport-19-commandments/

Cobo, C., & Moravec, J. W. (2011). *Aprendizaje invisible: Hacia una nueva ecología de la educación.* Barcelona: Laboratori de Mitjans Interactius / Publicacions i Edicions de la Universitat de Barcelona.

Cobo Romaní, C., & Pardo Kuklinski, H. (2007). *Planeta Web 2.0: Inteligencia colectiva o medios fast food.* Mexico City: FLACSO.

Cross, J. (2003). Informal learning - the other 80%. Retrieved from www.internettime.com/Learning/The%20Other%2080%25.htm

Dewey, J. (1915). *The school and society* (Revised ed.). Chicago: University of Chicago.

Drucker, P. F. (1969). *The age of discontinuity: Guidelines to our changing society.* New York: Harper & Row.

Drucker, P. F. (1985). Innovation and entrepreneurship: Practice and principles (1st ed.). New York: Harper & Row.

Freire, P. (2000). Pedagogy of the oppressed (30th anniversary ed.). New York: Continuum.

Gladstone, B. (Writer). (1999). The science in science fiction [Radio broadcast], Talk of the Nation: National Public Radio.

Godin, S. (2010). Linchpin: Are you indispensible? New York: Portfolio.

Harkins, A. M., & Moravec, J. W. (2006). Building a Leapfrog University v5.0. Education Futures. Retrieved from www.education-futures.com/2006/10/12/building-a-leapfrog-university-v50/

Herbert, B. (2010, October 9). Policy at its worst, New York Times, p. A21. Retrieved from www.ny-times.com/2010/10/09/opinion/09herbert.html

Hyatt, M. (2010, January 26). Book notes: An interview with Seth Godin. Retrieved from michaelhyatt.com/book-notes-an-interview-with-seth-godin.html

Ihanainen, P. (2010, September 4). [Personal communication on vocational teacher education in Finland].

Krauss, L. M., & Starkman, G. D. (2004). Universal limits on computation. arxiv.org/abs/astro-ph/0404510v2

Kurzweil, R. (1999). The age of spiritual machines: When computers exceed human intelligence. New York: Viking.

Kurzweil, R. (2005). The Singularity is near: When humans transcend biology. New York: Viking.

Mahiri, J. (2004). What they don't learn in school: Literacy in the lives of urban youth. New York: P. Lang.

Marzano, R. J. (2003). What works in schools: Translating research into action. Alexandria, Va.: Association for Supervision and Curriculum Development.

Meyer, M. (2010). The rise of the knowledge broker. Science Communication, 32(1), 118-127. doi: 10.1177/1075547009359797

Molist, M. (2010, February 25). Schank: "El 'e-learning' actual es la misma basura, pero en diferente sitio", Interview, El País. Retrieved from elpais.com/diario/2010/02/25/ciber-pais/1267068270_850215.html

Moore, G. E. (1965). Cramming more components onto integrated circuits. Electronics Magazine, 38(8).

Moravec, J. W. (2008a, November 20). Knowmads in Society 3.0. Education Futures. Retrieved from www.education-futures.com/2008/11/20/know-mads-in-society-30/

Moravec, J. W. (2008b). A new paradigm of knowledge production in higher education. On the Horizon, 16(3), 123-136. doi: 10.1108/10748120810901422

Moravec, J. W. (2008c). Toward Society 3.0: A New Paradigm for 21st century education. Paper presented at the ASOMEX Technology Conference, Monterrey, Mexico. www.slideshare.net/moravec/toward-society-30-a-new-paradigm-for-21st-century-education-presentation

Moravec, J. W. (2010, October 5). Review: Education Nation (by Milton Chen). Education Futures. Retrieved from www.educationfutures.com/2010/08/17/review-education-nation-by-milton-chen/

Moravec, J. W. (2012, July 16). The Singularity and schools: An interview with Vernor Vinge. Education Futures. Retrieved from www.educationfutures.com/2012/07/16/the-singularity-and-schools-an-interview-with-vernor-vinge/

Morgan, L. H. (1877). Ancient society. New York: H. Holt and company.

Polanyi, M. (1968). Personal knowledge: Towards a post-critical philosophy. Chicago: University of Chicago.

Robinson, K. (2001). Out of our minds: Learning to be creative. Oxford: Capstone.

Robinson, K., & Aronica, L. (2009). The element: How finding your passion changes everything. New York: Viking.

Rushkoff, D. (2013). Present shock: When everything happens now. New York: Penguin.

Schwartz, P., & Ogilvy, J. A. (1979). The emergent paradigm: Changing patterns of thought and belief. Menlo Park, CA: SRI International.

Small, G., & Vorgan, G. (2008). iBrain: Surviving the technological alteration of the modern mind. New York: HarperCollins.

Stiggins, R. J. (2008). An introduction to student-involved assessment for learning (5th ed.). Upper Saddle River, N.J.: Pearson/Merrill Prentice Hall.

Stiggins, R. J., Arter, J. A., Chappuis, J., & Chappuis, S. (2007). *Classroom assessment for student learning: Doing it right -- using it well* (Special ed.). Upper Saddle River, N.J.: Pearson Education, Inc.

TED. (Producer). (2010). Sir Ken Robinson: Bring on the learning revolution! Retrieved from www.ted.com/talks/sir_ken_robinson_bring_on_the_revolution.html

TED. (n.d.). About TED. Retrieved May 3, 2013, from www.ted.com/pages/view/id/5

Vinge, V. (1993). The Technological Singularity. Retrieved from www.kurzweilai.net/the-technological-singularity

Zenke, P. F. (2013). Education in "Present Shock" : An interview with Douglas Rushkoff. *Education Futures.* Retrieved from www.educationfutures.com/2013/05/03/education-in-present-shock-an-interview-with-douglas-rushkoff/

....

....

....

....

....

....

....

....

....

....

....

....

....

....

....

....

notes

NOTES

Good thinking!

notes

....

....

....

....

....

....

....

....

....

....

....

....

....

....

Skills and competencies for knowmadic workers

CRISTÓBAL COBO

'Learning how to learn becomes an opportunity to include a variety of learning experiences, including serendipitous conversations, experiments, and peer-based exchanges.'

'In today's complex and changing environment, the challenge is to build skills that allow young people to think critically and creatively, as well as to effectively process information, make decisions, manage conflict, and work in teams.'

'THE PROBLEM LIES NOT ONLY IN IDENTIFYING WHY EDUCATION FAILS, BUT ALSO IN HOW TO DESIGN SUCCESSFUL SOLUTIONS.'

CRISTÓBAL COBO

'THE "WALLED GARDEN" OF FORMAL EDUCATION SHOULD FIND MECHANISMS AND PRACTICES TO STIMULATE NEW FORMS AND MODES OF LEARNING, ENCOURAGING THE CREATION OF MORE SUITABLE EDUCATION PARADIGMS.'

'WHILE WE MIGHT NOT BE ABLE TO PREDICT THE FUTURE, WE CAN STILL CREATE A FUTURE IN WHICH WE ALL WANT TO LIVE.'

SUMMARY

SKILLS AND COMPETENCES FOR KNOWMADIC WORKERS
~ Cristóbal Cobo ~

This chapter is an expanded compilation of the discussions and ideas that arose following the publication of *Aprendizaje invisible*, that I wrote with John Moravec in 2011. This work contributes to a debate around the challenges facing education today. Instead of outlining a recipe of solutions for education (which lies far beyond my scope) the approach offered here enquires, explores, and outlines the conditions required to foster critical skills such as problem-solving, reflection, creativity, critical thinking, learning to learn, risk-taking, collaboration, and entrepreneurship.

I discuss five trends that can be used to explore the conditions necessary to ensure "multi-skilled profiles" and "multi-contextual learning practices" for an expanded understanding of education:

- The mismatch between formal education and the challenges of the innovation society (informal and flexible learning approaches);
- The shift from what we learn to how we learn (life-long, self-learning, and learning to learn);
- The fluctuating relationship between digital technologies and content (ICT and critical thinking skills and new literacies);
- The changing conceptions of space-time and a life-long learning environment (which is rarely time or context dependent); and,
- The development of soft skills (global, tacit, and social).

The challenge now, as always, is to bring these ideas to action, and to explore the conditions for triggering those "multi-skilled profiles" which are relevant for stimulating a mode of learning that happens anytime and anywhere. If a knowmad is able to learn and unlearn continuously, then the mismatches described in this chapter will only form part of an endless but resilient process of adaptation. It is therefore desirable that the "walled garden" of formal education should find mechanisms and practices to stimulate new forms and modes of learning, encouraging the creation of more suitable education paradigms. At the same time, individuals should embrace and share their own strategies to learn continuously.

Without better curriculum, better teaching, and better tests, the emphasis on '21st-century skills' will be superficial. (Rotherham and Willingham 2010)

In 2011, John Moravec and I released a book entitled *Invisible learning* (originally published in Spanish as *Aprendizaje invisible*). The book was openly accessible under a Creative Commons license, and it was downloaded thousands of times by people from all around the world. The volume contributed to a worldwide debate about the challenges faced by education today. We, as authors, were lucky enough to give talks in dozens of universities (among other institutions) in numerous countries around the world. This was an extraordinary opportunity to discuss and expand on many of the topics we analyzed in the book, as people from different cultures and nationalities, ages and experiences, shared their views on how to think critically and creatively about education. The chapter that follows is not a summary of *Aprendizaje invisible*, but an expanded compilation of the discussions and ideas that arose following its publication. I thereby hope to share ideas that can contribute towards an expanded understanding of contemporary education.

Provision of a cross-cutting education that enables citizens to flexibly and proactively respond to change overtime from a life-long learning society, as Redecker et al. (2010, pp. 28–30) have suggested, is one of the challenges that educational systems need to address. However, as Richard Rowe from the Open Learning Exchange International once told me, the problem lies not only in identifying why education fails, but also in how to design successful solutions. Instead of outlining a recipe of solutions for education (which lies far beyond my scope) the approach offered here will be to enquire, explore and outline the conditions required to foster critical skills such as problem-solving, reflection, creativity, critical thinking, learning to learn, risk-taking, collaboration, and entrepreneurship. In this chapter, I discuss five trends that can be used to explore the conditions necessary to ensure "multi-skilled profiles" and "multi-contextual learning practices" for an expanded understanding of education. These five trends can be summarized as follows:

1 The mismatch between formal education and the challenges of an innovation-based society (informal and flexible learning approaches);

2 The shift from *what* we learn to *how* we learn (life-long, self-learning, and learning to learn);

3 The fluctuating relationship between digital technologies and content (ICT and critical thinking skills and new literacies);

4 The changing conceptions of space-time and a life-long learning environment (which is rarely time or context dependent); and,

5 The development of soft skills (global, tacit and social).

Before I analyze some of the strategic conditions that are necessary to foster the development of the above key skills, I provide two relevant definitions

elaborated by the European Centre for the Development of Vocational Training (Tissot, 2004) and published in the European multilingual glossary:

1 **Skill:** "the knowledge and experience needed to perform a specific task or job."

2 **Competence:** the "ability to apply knowledge, know-how and skills in a habitual or changing situation."

This differentiation and complementarity is important to consider. While this chapter devotes particular attention to the development of skills, it also addresses the application of skills in changing situations and through the combination of disciplines.

THE MISMATCH BETWEEN FORMAL EDUCATION AND THE CHALLENGES OF AN INNOVATION-BASED SOCIETY

In their book, *The new division of labor: How computers are creating the next job market*, Frank Levy and Richard Murnane (2004) analyze the most universally needed competencies in a modern economy in a longitudinal study spanning the period of 1960 to 2000. They make reference to the fact that "declining portions of the labor force are engaged in jobs that consist primarily of routine cognitive work and routine manual labor—the types of tasks that are easiest to program computers to do. Growing proportions of the nation's labor force are engaged in jobs that emphasize expert thinking or complex communication—tasks that computers cannot do" (Levy & Murnane, 2004, pp. 53–54). They also explain the importance of the "expert thinking" profile of workers who are capable of working in a changing environment using skills such as creativity, communication, collaboration, and problem-solving.

It is possible that Levy and Murnane's vision of the decline of "routine cognitive work" and "routine manual labor" will not be particularly surprising to contemporary readers. There is a large body of academic literature that analyzes the changing structure of the world of work, and the necessity of new skills and qualifications to support the knowledge economy. For instance, Jimenez (2006) notes that that this concern has existed in the United States for decades: "Job tasks requiring problem-solving and communication skills have grown steadily since the 1970s in the United States while manual and routine cognitive tasks have declined" (p. 72). Attention has therefore been focused on the novelty of this changing nature of worker profiles, rather than on efforts to make these changes happen.

Economics and education scholars have been largely studying and exploring how to better match the needs of employers with suitable graduate profiles. One of the main complexities of this match (or mismatch) between

the worlds of work and education is the convergence of various elements, including the performance of universities and training institutions, the changing requirements of the productive sector, mutual coordination between training and the labor sector, and differing levels of employability and competitiveness between different countries and regions worldwide. In other words, a better understanding of the changing trends in division of labor as envisioned by Levy and Murnane entails an interplay between – and integration of – at least the higher education sector, the production sector, and public policy frameworks.

This is not a new concern, and it is not limited to any specific nation. Many classic works have explained and illustrated why it is important to explore a more appropriate design of educational systems, ones that better suit the demands of the changing, global economy. A report that can be considered a "classic" in this respect is *A nation at risk: The imperative for educational reform* (Gardner et al. 1983), which, in the early 1980s, compared the performance of U.S. students and the U.S. educational system with that of other industrialized nations. In their work, considered a landmark event in modern U.S. educational history, Gardner and his colleagues highlighted the importance of stimulating skills such as comprehending, interpreting, evaluating, and using what is read; applying scientific knowledge to everyday life; understanding the computer as an information, computation, and communication device; and computational and problem solving skills, science, social studies, foreign language, and the arts.

However, as might be suspected, this is not the end of the story. Today, and still with reference to the U.S. educational context, various initiatives have re-branded the suggestions of Gardner et al. (1983) as "21st century skills." The "Partnership for 21st Century Skills" (P21) is an example of a national concern about skills development, but which stresses the importance of modern technologies in disseminating "new" capabilities within the education sector. The Partnership is self-defined as a "national organization that advocates for 21st century readiness for every student [as] the United States continues to compete in a global economy that demands innovation," and explains the importance of transforming education, developing students' educational skills such as creativity and innovation, critical thinking and problem solving, communication and collaboration, and information, media and technology skills.

It is interesting to note the similarities between the approach taken by the *A nation at risk* report (1983) and what is promoted by the P21 report (2012) as a way of "transforming" education, despite the almost 30 years that separate the two proposals. With very little difference between them, both

U.S. initiatives push for an education that provides more relevance to a whole "new" set of skills that students will need. Before drawing any conclusions about the unchanged rhetoric surrounding these "new" skills, it is reasonable to ask: What is missed? Where is the novelty in this "skills approach"? In other words, *what happened in the U.S. educational institutions (and other regions of the world) during the last three decades?* Is this just a matter of describing more appropriate skills, or are deeper changes required? Will the Americans (or others) be rediscovering the same problems in three decades' time?

When the phenomenon of the education-jobs mismatch is discussed, it is important to identify and differentiate between two kind of incompatibilities: a skills mismatch and a qualifications mismatch. An OECD (2011) report suggests the following definitions to illustrate the difference between these concepts:

- **Skills mismatch:** Discrepancy between the skills – both specific and general – possessed by a worker and the skills required by their job.
- **Qualifications mismatch:** Discrepancy between the highest qualifications held by a worker and the qualifications required by their job.

The same OECD study explains that most of the literature has so far focused on qualification levels. Too few studies

Figure 2. Do you think you were given the required skills at school/
college to find and hold on to a sustainable job in the present
employment market? (5 = yes, very much so / 0 = not at all).

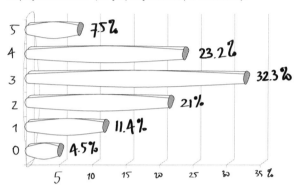

have investigated the role played by field of study and other factors in explaining qualification mismatches, or explored underlying skill discrepancies. That is why I present here an analysis that discusses the importance of these "skills mismatches" with special relevance of other contextual variables. In other words, I discuss how to better stimulate the development of multi-skilled profiles in the coming generation of professionals and how to better understand the importance of those multi-contextual learning practices that foster the creation of new capacities and proficiencies.

Between April and June of 2010, the Generation Europe Foundation conducted paper surveys and online interviews with young people in the EU, who were between the ages of 18 and 30. 7,062 responses were received: 95% were aged 18-30, 62% were female and 38% male (Generation Europe Foundation, 2010, p. 8). One of the questions addressed by the study was whether the new generation (defined as people between the ages of 19 and 29) considered that they had received the necessary tools and guidance for entering the employment market.

The study showed that less than one third of the people surveyed believed that they were definitely given (or were currently being given) the required skills at school or college. One in six believed they had not been given the right skills, and the majority were somewhat uncertain.

This is worthy of a deeper analysis. The fact that less than one third of the respondents believed they were given the required skills raises questions about the contributions of education, and how well prepared young people are in meeting the demands of the labor market. Nevertheless, it is important to mention that the report also noted significant national differences. The proportion believing they had missed out on preparation for the employment market (0 or 1 out of 5) was particularly high in Italy and Greece, and lowest in Germany and the UK (Generation Europe Foundation, 2010, p. 8). The study adds a clear message for education policy makers: hands-on work experience could go a long way to addressing the skills gap that prevents young people from landing their first job (Generation Europe Foundation, 2010, p. 9). This is exactly what we mean by the idea of "multi-contextual learning practices," an idea I will come back to later on. Here it is important to distinguish, as the OECD has presented, the differences between a skills mismatch and a qualifications mismatch.

As the Generation Europe Foundation's survey illustrates, access to education or training cannot be correlated directly with the acquisition of the particular skills required by the labor market. Excerpts from the "next generation" interviews include:

- "Most of the universities give far too much theoretical preparation and too little preparation about how to face the real world of work!"
- "Most students don't know anything about the business world and how to get the right preparation for job interviews."
- "Since I experienced the great difference between reality in my job and the theory that I was taught at university, I would suggest having a field study, practical experience as an obligatory part of the process."
- "Too many times I hear people lamenting after they graduate that they had to learn almost everything again at the work place, because the knowledge they got at university (or high school) was useless."
- "Universities can do a better job of career advice. Many students still don't know what they want to do when they graduate. So, the more options you have, the more flexible you become. This poses a real risk for would-be employers – who wants to invest in a person who can change his mind tomorrow?" (Generation Europe Foundation 2010, pp. 9–11)

The OECD's (2011) report described possible types of mismatch such as being over-skilled or over-qualified, as well as being under-skilled or under-qualified. Today, there is clear and worldwide evidence that an increasing number of people have access to higher education (Cobo and Moravec, 2011). Nevertheless, that growing number of people with higher education degrees cannot, and should not, be understood as representative of a reduction in the previously indicated mismatches. In many cases, as the OECD (2011) report indicates, the increasing number of professionals is resulting in an increasing number of underemployed workers.

The OECD's *Employment outlook* (2011, p.195) emphasizes that the underlying assumption of many papers in the academic literature, and most articles in the press, about over-qualification is that what is being measured is a discrepancy between the skills of the individual – often a young graduate – and those required by the job they hold. In fact, while qualifications might at first seem to be one of the closest proxies for skills, they are an imperfect one for several reasons:

1   At each qualification level, student performance varies significantly and so does field of study, particularly for tertiary-level graduates;
2   Qualifications only reflect skills learned in formal education and certified training;
3   Skills learned on the job through labor market experience are not measured; and,
4   Some of the skills reflected in qualifications may deteriorate over time if they are not used or kept up-to-date.

Despite these differences between qualifications and skills, the OECD (2011) states that:

Qualification mismatch is clearly inefficient and should be of serious policy concern as it implies either that there has been over- or under-investment in education and training – e.g. there is a discrepancy between the shares of complex jobs and highly-qualified workers – or that workers and jobs do not match efficiently along the qualification dimension or both. (p. 221)

The same report explains that it is important to recognize that skills formation and the demand for skills – as well as the process of matching them – are undergoing long-term changes somewhat independently. The challenges still remain almost unchanged, i.e. the necessity to have educational systems that better prepare people for the world of work, not only in terms of academic or technical knowledge, but also in terms of situational skills. However, this cannot be seen as the exclusive problem for those who are about to start working or those who are looking for their first job. This is also relevant in terms of life-long learning for those workers who want to better suit their company.

The mismatch should be seen as an interdependent and complex phenomenon that can be solved by better articulating the coordination between the work and education sectors. However, the idea of a "better articulation" shouldn't simply be read as adding more courses or years to the curriculum, but as having a better idea of the importance of the "multi-skilled profiles" that are created by multi-contextual learning practices. Strengthening the connection between schools and universities, work, and "real life" is one of the big challenges. In that sense, it is central to have an education system that is more relevant to work, and that facilitates a more articulated transition (Jimenez, 2006, p. 76). In the following section, I explore "multi-skilled profiles" and "multi-contextual learning practices," and discuss how they can be better interrelated.

THE SHIFT FROM WHAT WE LEARN TO HOW WE LEARN

Keeping in mind that it is important not to confuse or ignore the difference between a "skills mismatch" and a "qualifications mismatch," the development of learning practices is analyzed here in a more comprehensive way. Note that "thinking skills" will be regarded in this analysis as complex skills (not basic ones) in different contexts and various environments.

Labaree (2008) criticizes those who habitually use education as a buzz-word for the cause of all of society's problems. He argues that there is a puzzling paradox in "educationalizing" society's social problems, "even though schools have repeatedly proven that they are an ineffective mechanism for solving these problems." For instance, if there is a concern about unemployment, education can easily be blamed as the main cause; if people are underemployed, education can also be blamed for being inefficient. In other words, "educationalization" is often assumed to be a shortcut to the solution of almost any problem; "[w]ith the tacit understanding that by educationalizing these problem-solving efforts we are seeking a solution that is more formal than substantive" (Labaree, 2008). In order to confront the educationalizing of society's problems, Labaree opens up the possibility of a broader perspective of the learning practice beyond the context of formal education.

A broader understanding of learning must also accommodate the concept of life-long learning, otherwise referred to as continuous learning, life-long learning, life learning, ubiquitous learning, non-standard learning, adult learning, mobile learning, community or peer based learning, etc. All these new and old concepts that suggest more flexible ways of learning have one common denominator which is important to highlight: the strategies used to leverage learning are equally, or even more, important than the content acquired during the learning process. Here, I propose that attention should be paid not only to formal learning, but also to more flexible approaches based on informal education, which can help us to conceive of learning as a dynamic and active process that goes beyond the framework of formal education. Under this perspective, "multi-contextual learning practices" can be considered as a flexible and suitable approaches that should be taken into account.

Informal education can be understood as the learning that goes on in daily life that we undertake and organize for ourselves. Informal learning works through conversation, and the exploration and gaining of experience in changing environments. This contradicts the idea of formal education, which tends to take place in special settings such as schools. However, we should not get too tied up with a consideration of physical setting: formal education can operate in a wide range of settings, often within the same day (George Williams College & YMCA, 2011).

Obviously "informal learning" cannot be understood as an activity instead of "formal learning." It has to be seen as a supplement that we develop

permanently. Informal learning is a useful approach when we think of learning as a continuous, changing and not necessarily certifiable process. The benefit of these flexible approaches is not only the possibility of learning from multiple spaces but also the possibility to develop different kinds of skills and expertise. The challenge now is to find the mechanisms to develop skills, capacities, and techniques that facilitate learning to learn in a continuous, incremental, and smart process, without the restrictions of any specific discipline or teaching program.

Dede (2010) refers to this idea when he writes about *scientific learning*. He suggests that individuals need to learn to "think scientifically," and that in order to do so, they need to understand the importance of anomalous results in an experiment. He proposes that what will activate new explorations and the possibility to reach new knowledge is the capacity to inquire, investigate and continuously create new methods of discovery, through what he terms "thinking scientifically" – i.e., the aptitude to explore beyond the information available. Rearticulating Labaree's concept of "educationalizing" all the problems of society, it is essential today to have an expanded understanding of learning. However, not everything can be attributed to the quality of an education system. Any individual with a minimum set of knowledge and skills can develop their own strategies to enhance their learning based on different contexts and experiences. In this sense, it is fundamental to create relevance for those strategies and mechanisms that help people to learn within - but also outside - the institutional education framework. This flexibility will provide more relevance for the role of the individual as a continuous self-learning "node" in a networked society.

In terms of learning outcomes, Rotherham & Willingham (2010) add that it is important not to oversimplify the relationship between content and skills:

If you believe that skills and knowledge are separate, you are likely to draw two incorrect conclusions. First, because content is readily available in many locations but thinking skills reside in the learner's brain, it would seem clear that if we must choose between them, skills are essential, whereas content is merely desirable. Second, if skills are independent of content, we could reasonably conclude that we can develop these skills through the use of any content. (p. 18)

Dede (2010) also supplies the criticism that, in formal education, "knowledge is separated from skills and presented as revealed truth, not as an understanding that is discovered and constructed." He explains that this separation results in students learning data about a topic rather than learning how to extend their comprehension beyond the information made available for assimilation.

A different understanding of how knowledge is co-created and continuously re-constructed will stimulate not only memorizing of data, but also stimulation of the skills required to "think scientifically." Here the challenge will be how to create more relevance for the development of these thinking skills, which embrace and stimulate new learning potential. The aim is to combine teaching students how to think, and also to transform the idea that content is to be learned (or memorized in many cases) and that skills are developed only within the classroom. Targeting *how* to learn, and not only *what* to learn, stresses the relevance of being adaptable as well as thinking scientifically in different spaces, times, and contexts beyond the boundaries of traditional formal education.

Dede (2010) adds that the development of "thinking skills" highlights the ability to rapidly filter increasing amounts of incoming data in order to extract information that is valuable for decision making. He argues that this is a "contextual" capability, which helps to separate signal from noise in a potentially overwhelming flood of incoming data. This provides a perspective that will help the individual to perform better in a disordered and "miscellaneous" (to use Weinberger's concept, 2007) environment of information overload.

THE FLUCTUATING RELATIONSHIP BETWEEN DIGITAL TECHNOLOGIES AND CONTENT

In a lecture, Google chairman Eric Schmidt delivered a critique of the UK's education system, stating that it had failed to capitalize on the UK's record of innovation in science and engineering. Schmidt said the country that invented the computer was "throwing away [its] great computer heritage" by failing to teach programming in schools. "I was flabbergasted to learn that today computer science isn't even taught as standard in UK schools," he said. "Your IT curriculum focuses on teaching how to use software, but gives no insight into how it's made." (Shepherd, 2011)

Moravec, in an interview with Yu (2010), which explored the use of technologies in learning practices, described his point of view. He argued that technologies should be used to help individuals learn how to think, and not to tell them what to think:

I believe we need to engineer new technologies to help them HOW to learn, not WHAT to learn. Our school systems have focused on WHAT for centuries. Likewise, we see too many educational technologies focus on the WHAT as well (i.e., pushing content rather than new idea generation). WHAT technologies are great for producing factory workers, but for creatives and innovators, we need to focus more on HOW to learn. The rapidly changing world demands no less. Students need to build capacities for continuous learning, unlearning, and relearning to be competitive globally. So, I believe that the technologies that address the HOW question will become the key for educational success in the remainder of the 21st century. (Yu, 2010)

Moravec's vision can be used to rethink how information and communication technologies (ICT) are used, but it also suggests a broader understanding of learning itself. He emphasizes the importance of learning from changing practices and spaces. In other words, the "how" we learn also becomes an opportunity to include a variety of learning experiences such as experiments, non-planned conversations, peer-based exchanges, peer observation, training, etc. A "multi-skilled profile" refers to the capability of taking advantage of different opportunities for learning, compiling, reprocessing and translating different content into changing contexts.

Levy and Murnane (2004) discuss the kinds of jobs that are likely to endure, and those that will eventually disappear. To do so, they explored the following questions:

1   What kinds of tasks do humans perform better than computers?
2   What kinds of tasks do computers perform better than humans?

After their analysis, they conclude that there are three main types of work that cannot be described in rules, and that would therefore be extremely difficult to be undertaken by non-human intelligence. These tasks can be summarized as:

1 Identifying and solving new problems (if the problem is new, there is no rules-based solution to program).
2 Engaging in complex communication —verbal and non-verbal— with other people in jobs like leading, negotiating, teaching, and selling.
3 Doing many "simple" physical tasks and jobs that apparently are trivial but that are also extremely difficult to program, such as making sense of, adapting or transferring knowledge to new problems. (Levy & Murnane, 2004)

Dede (2010) mentions that 21st century skills are different from 20th century skills, primarily due to the emergence of very sophisticated ICTs. The question that now arises is whether these technologies can be used to foster creativity (and other critical thinking skills) or only to perform routine tasks.

Many teachers disapprove of the use of Wikipedia and other online open educational resources due to a concern that students can copy and paste content. It is fair to say that if an educator sets questions that can be adequately answered merely by copying and pasting, it wouldn't be surprising that the skills promoted might be routine ones (i.e. search, find, copy, paste). However, if teachers set questions to which definitive answers do not exist – that is, which may never exist on Wikipedia or anywhere else - then students will be encouraged to explore and create their own explanations or analyses. This approach of asking new, creative questions goes much closer to promoting the development of expert or critical thinking skills.

Current approaches to technology use in educational environments largely reflect the application of ICTs as a means of increasing the effectiveness of traditional tasks. That can be understood as 20th century, instructional approaches like enhancing productivity through tools such as word processors, e-mail communication, participation in asynchronous discussions, and expanding access to information via Web browsers or video. All of these methods, according to Dede (2010), have proven useful in conventional educational environments. However, the full potential of ICTs for individual and collective expression, experience, and interpretation can go far beyond this point if their use is appropriately stimulated and supported. Dede adds that the use of technological applications is generally excluded from testing environments and processes – i.e. that students' capacities to use tools, applications, and media effectively are not being assessed. As discussed above, valid, reliable, and practical assessments of knowledge and skills in action are needed in order to improve and promote "multi-contextual practices."

These tests should not only assess students' ICT skills, but also their ability to use these skills to solve complex problems involving research, communication, information management, and presentations. These problems should involve both technical skills and learning skills, such as "finding things out," "developing ideas," and "exchanging and sharing information" (Dede, 2010).

In their study, *The future of learning: Preparing for change*, Redecker et al. (2010, pp. 28–30) from the Institute for Prospective Technological Studies compiled a set of studies that aim to improve understandings of the coming role of ICTs in teaching and learning practices. Relevant ideas they presented include:

- Technology will be one of the main drivers for changing job structures and requirements, and will thus determine which skills people need to acquire.
- Technology not only affects what we will need to learn, it also affects how we will learn in the future.
- The key to adequately preparing learners for life in a digital world is to redesign education itself around participative, digitally enabled collaboration within and beyond the individual educational institution.
- Learning in education and training (E&T) institutions will be based on the principles of self-learning, networked learning, connectivity and interactivity, and collective credibility.
- Pedagogy will use inductive and de-centered methods for knowledge generation, and open source education will prevail. Learning institutions will be characterized by horizontal structures, mobilizing networks and flexible scalability.
- There are interrelated "signposts" for the future of education, which indicate a set of challenges and/ or opportunities for E&T. These signposts are technological immersion; personalized learning paths; knowledge skills for service-based economies; global integration of

systems, resources, and cultures; and, aligning E&T with economic needs and demands.

- All citizens will need to continuously update and enhance their skills throughout their lives.
- Individuals will need to re-create themselves as resilient systems with flexible, open, and adaptive infrastructures, which engage all citizens and re-connect with society; schools will become dynamic, community-wide systems and networks that have the capacity to renew themselves in the context of change.

As a compilation of previously presented perspectives, their work is relevant in re-conceptualizing the use of technologies - not as tools that reinforce the development of routine manual or intellectual practices, but as devices that can contribute to better application of skills and knowledge in changing and unpredictable situations. In addition, it is important to have a clear vision of which ICT practices can stimulate the development of higher order skills such as distributed production of knowledge; knowledge translation; distributed collaborative work; workforce training, re-skilling and up-skilling; and, adaptability, resilience and networking.

As previously discussed, informal and multi-contextual learning practices are considered strategic components for an individual's development. Therefore, ICTs are powerful tools to facilitate life-long learning anywhere and anytime. It is important that ICTs are used not only as devices to receive formal education (such as in school computer class or e-learning), but also as an opportunity to develop more versatile and adaptable learning not restricted to any formal education system.

Access, the ability to modify, and easier modes to share content are key benefits provided by digital technologies. The challenge is to develop the capabilities to access, evaluate and select relevant information. When these essential capabilities are developed – critical evaluation and expertise in locating relevant information – there are virtually unlimited possibilities for new learning.

It is important to understand the skills related to the use of ICTs as competencies that help to create and re-create knowledge in different contexts and formats. These e-competencies (as they will be referred to in what follows), are "meta-competencies that denote the interaction of different skills and knowledge (multi-literacies or hyper-literacies), which are constituted by five underlying concepts: e-awareness; technological literacy; informational literacy; digital literacy; and, media literacy. The relevance of one or more of the underlying concepts will depend on the context and the particular needs of each specific user" (Cobo, 2009, p.23). This definition embraces cognitive abilities as well as technical proficiencies (to create a multi-skilled profile). It encapsulates the idea that the development of e-competencies is enriched by the continuous interaction and connection between knowledge and experience. Also, it suggests that one of the distinctive characteristics of these e-competencies is their "transferability" between different contexts or formats.

THE CHANGING CONCEPTIONS OF SPACE-TIME AND THE LIFE-LONG LEARNING ENVIRONMENT

In discussing the concept of the Information Age, Castells noted how we are reconceptualizing our ideas about time and space:

As with all historical transformations, the emergence of a new social structure is necessarily linked to the redefinition of the material foundations of life, time and space. Time and space are related, in society as in nature. Their meaning, and manifestations in social practice, evolve throughout histories and across cultures [...] I propose the hypothesis that the network society, as the dominant structure emerging in the Information Age, is organized around new forms of time and space: timeless time, the space of flows. (Castells, 1997, p. 12)

For more than two centuries, formal education has been organized around industrial principles. Weyand (1925) talked about the harmony between public schools and the "industrial machine" in the mid-1920s: "Industrial education is a method of experimentation for the purpose of finding out what adjustments can be made to bring the culture of the public school into harmony with the culture of machine industry and its accompanying organization" (p. 656).

Rifkin (2010) explains that this idea of an education shaped under the old industrial paradigm is not a matter of the past; he argues that it is still a current problem: "Unfortunately, our system today is still largely mired in those outdated assumptions. The classroom is a microcosm of the factory system." He criticizes the current (United States) educational system, saying that it has been unable to address the challenges posed by a globalized society: something that sounds very close to what we founded in the report, *A nation at risk* (1983).

The obsession with hyper-fragmentation and standardization is probably an industrial-era heritage that is still broadly adopted in the current education systems. Nowadays, this Fordist-Taylorist-rooted education can be seen in examples such as uniform rates of assessment; similar mechanisms of incentives (qualification and certification); content disconnects between courses; distribution of classes in equal time intervals (usually of 45 minutes); and, row seating in classrooms, a very clear vertical hierarchy where a small group dictates the performance of the rest. In a nutshell, it is a structure designed to implement an extremely mechanical and homogeneous treatment of the formal learning process (de Bary, 2010).

In this context, the concepts proposed by Castells' "timeless time" and "space of flows" suggest a different approach, and one that is especially relevant for new learning frameworks. We have referred already to the importance of envisaging a more flexible (and adaptable) understanding of education. Today, more than ever, "timeless time"

and a "space of flows" are observable among the youngest generation, who use ICTs at any moment and in any space.

Time and location are therefore not a limitation, at least at the theoretical level. Inevitably, this becomes an opportunity to expand learning throughout one's life, as well as to continuously develop new skills in changing contexts. Doubtless these ideas can enrich learning, as well as open up possibilities for non-traditional learning experiences. Since the publication of *Lessons of experience* (1988), the Center for Creative Leadership has continued to support for the belief that upwards of 70% of all learning development occurs through on-the-job experience. This phenomenon has become known as the "70-20-10" rule (McCall, Lombardo, and Morrison, 1988), which describes how learning occurs:

- 70% from real life and on-the-job experience, tasks and problem solving. This is the most important aspect of any learning and development plan.
- 20% from relationships, feedback, and from observing and working with role models.
- 10% from formal training opportunities.

Arguably the "measurability" of what we learn in specific contexts is a matter of discussion, particularly if we consider "tacit" knowledge. Nevertheless, the bottom line of this rule is that the our perception, as well as our practical use, of "space" and "time" have been changing dramatically.

While this is not a new concept (Lindeman, 1926), life-long and life-wide learning can be seen as the central learning paradigm for the future, and it is likely that learning strategies and pedagogical approaches will undergo dramatic changes. Redecker et al. (2010) suggest that teachers and trainers will need to be trained to support learning that takes place in many environments—at home, at school, and in the workplace. Rotherham and Willingham (2010) add that education faces enormous challenges, and they insist on the importance of teaching skills in context.

In addition, life-long learning not only describes and expands learning over space and time, it also describes the need to adopt more flexible methods of assessing, recognizing and translating knowledge and skills into different contexts. From the life-long learning perspective, Redecker et al. (2010, pp. 10 and 28) explain that learning takes place across a number of different "venues" and involves mixed-age groups in many different configurations. The challenges for life-long learning can be organized into three areas:

- Promoting a rapid and more **fluent transition from school to work** in order to reduce the barriers between the worlds of education and work;
- Facilitating **re-entry to the labor market**, especially in terms of tackling long-term unemployment; and,
- Focusing on **permanent re-skilling to enable all citizens to keep their competencies updated**, and to quickly respond and adjust to possibly fast changing work environments.

Undoubtedly, this perspective offers a variety of possibilities in terms of up-skilling and re-skilling, which can be used today to minimize some of the problems generated by a skills mismatch. In an environment of rapidly changing labor market demand, as well as an imprecise occupational environment, the acquisition of academic degrees alone is not sufficient to ensure that workers' skills fit well with job requirements. The OECD (2011) adds that "upgrade training could help counter skill obsolescence while re-training for a different occupation could be the best solution for workers displaced from declining sectors" (p. 221).

In many instances, opportunities for

retraining in high-growth occupations and pathways back into the education system could play a crucial role in addressing skills mismatches and shortages. The availability of accessible retraining options would also allow the workforce to re- or up-skill. More flexible features, such as the ones suggested below (OECD, 2011, p. 220), could make the return to learning easier for adults:

1   A modular structure, allowing learners to take only the parts of a course they need to re-qualify;
2   High-quality training systems to provide learning credits for skills that are transferable between fields/occupations; and,
3   Part-time learning opportunities for those who want to continue working.

In the knowledge society, skills accumulation cannot end with formal education. A more comprehensive life-long learning vision is essential to ensure that new skills are acquired throughout one's careers, and that skills are kept up to date and compatible with the framework of a rapidly evolving labor market. Here, the recognition of non-formal and informal learning may help to reduce the wage penalty faced by the under-qualified due to a lack of formal recognition of their competencies. Measures that recognize non-formal and informal learning can provide value to individuals at various stages of their working lives. The need for life-long skills development calls for employers provide on-the-job training, pathways back into the education system, and cost-effective training as part of active labor market policies for the unemployed (OECD, 2011, pp. 195-221).

Finally, from a formal education perspective, a high-quality education system must improve the relevance of school curricula by teaching students the practical knowledge, thinking, and behavioral skills demanded by the labor market, using teaching methods that facilitate the blending of academic and vocational curricula. Jimenez (2006, pp. 74 and 96) also mentions the importance of strengthening the connection between schools and the local economy in order to facilitate the school-to-work transition and to boost economic development.

THE DEVELOPMENT OF SOFT SKILLS

Thorndike defined social intelligence as, "[the] ability to understand others and act wisely in human relations" (Thorndike, 1920). He argued that social intelligence is different from academic ability, and that it is a key element in what makes people successful, and, most importantly, happy in life (Shalini, 2009). He based his theory on the following three facets of intelligence:

1 **Abstract intelligence:** pertaining to the ability to understand and manage ideas.

2 **Mechanical intelligence:** pertaining to the ability to understand and manage concrete objects.

3 **Social intelligence:** pertaining to the ability to understand and manage people.

Almost a century later, Goleman popularized another concept very close to the idea of social intelligence. He (in collaboration with Boyatzis, and McKee, 2004, pp. 30-31) focused on emotional intelligence as a wide array of competencies and skills that drive leadership performance. In their work, the authors summarized twenty-five competencies into four key domains:

1 **Self-awareness:** the ability to read one's emotions and recognize their impact while using gut feelings to guide decisions (often overlooked in business settings). It plays a crucial role in empathy, or sensing how someone else sees a situation; it also includes self-assessment and self-confidence.

2 **Self-management:** the ability to control one's emotions and impulses and adapt to changing circumstances. It also embraces self-control,

conscientiousness, adaptability, initiative and achievement-drive.

3 **Social awareness:** the ability to sense, understand, and react to others' emotions while comprehending social networks. It includes listening and understanding other people's perspectives.

4 **Relationship management:** the ability to inspire, influence, and develop others while managing conflict. It also involves conflict management, influence, communication, teamwork ,and collaboration.

In 2011, the Institute for the Future (IFTF) and the University of Phoenix Research Institute (UPRI) jointly identified 10 skills that they considered to be vital for the workforce by 2020. The study classified the key proficiencies and abilities required across different jobs and work settings. This prospective analysis provides an overview of the shifting landscape of skills that will be required over the next decade (Davies, Fidler, and Gorbis, 2011).

1 **Sense-making:** the ability to determine the deeper meaning or significance of what is being expressed.

2 **Social intelligence:** the ability to connect to others in a deep and direct way, and to sense and stimulate reactions and desired interactions.

3 **Novel and adaptive thinking:** proficiency at thinking and coming up with solutions and responses beyond those that are rule-based.

4 **Cross-cultural competency:** the

ability to operate in different cultural settings in a truly globally connected world. Given a worker's skill set could see that person posted in any number of locations, he/she needs to be able to operate in whatever environment that person finds himsef/herself in.

5 **Computational thinking:** the ability to translate vast amounts of data into abstract concepts and to understand data-based reasoning.

6 **New Media Literacy:** the ability to critically assess and develop content that uses new media forms, and to leverage these media for persuasive communication.

7 **Transdisciplinarity:** literacy in and ability to understand concepts across multiple disciplines.

8 **Design mindset:** the ability to represent and develop tasks and work processes for desired outcomes.

9 **Cognitive load management:** the ability to discriminate and filter information in terms of importance, and to understand how to maximize cognitive functioning using a variety of tools and techniques.

10 **Virtual collaboration:** the ability to work productively, drive engagement, and demonstrate presence as a member of a virtual team.

Regardless of any actual capacity for

foresight, these three different perspectives (Thorndike, 1920; Goleman, Boyatzis, and McKee, 2004; IFTF and UPRI, 2011) illustrate the importance of developing a multi-skills profile that includes such capacities as trans-disciplinary knowledge, life-long learning development, knowledge translation, improvement of new literacies, and adaptability (understood as a continuous reassessment of the required skills). By no means can these approaches be considered as models to be applied to all situations, regardless of context or circumstances. Different frameworks and tasks will demand the development of specific abilities. However, they illustrate the necessity to promote a set of more flexible and versatile skills. In addition, these approaches highlight the importance of soft skills as key tools for human capital development.

Daniels (2011) explains that, "*soft skills*, or social behavioral skills, must be learned through understanding and practice. *Functional* skills may typically be acquired in a logical and systematic way, while management and interpersonal skills must be acquired through training, coaching and practice." Functional skills (such as driving a car, speaking a foreign language, using a computer or specific software) are easy to measure, assess, and certify. By contrast, the soft skills (also referred to as "people skills" or "social skills") that are needed for everyday life are typically hard to observe, quantify, or measure. Hurrell (2009) noted that the soft skills involve "interpersonal and intrapersonal abilities to facilitate mastered performance in particular contexts" (p. 397)

Dede (2010) created a compilation of educational policy frameworks from different nations that note the importance of soft skills. Based on his work, I present a compendium of key soft skills:

1 **Critical-thinking:** problem-solving skills; managing complexity; higher-order thinking; sound reasoning; and, planning and managing activities to develop a solution or complete a project.

2 **Searching, synthesizing and disseminating information:** collecting and analyzing data to identify solutions and/or make informed decisions; using models and simulations to explore complex systems and issues; and, transferring individual understanding to real world situations.

3 **Creativity and innovation skills:** curiosity, and using existing knowledge to generate new ideas, products or processes.

4 **Collaboration skills:** networking; negotiation; collecting distributed knowledge; and, contributing to project teams to produce original works or to solve problems.

5 **Contextual learning skills:** adaptability; and, developing cultural understanding and global awareness by engaging with learners of other cultures.

6 **Self-direction:** risk taking and entrepreneurship.

7 **Communication skills:** creating original works as a means of personal or group expression; communicating information and ideas effectively to multiple audiences using a variety of media and formats; and, meaningfully sampling and remixing media content.

As has been described in this chapter, in today's complex and changing environment, the challenge is to build skills that allow young people to think critically and creatively, as well as to effectively process information, make decisions, manage conflict, and work in teams (Jimenez, 2006, p. 75). The OECD adds (2011), "Critical thinking and problem solving, for example, have been components of human progress throughout history, from the development of early tools, to agricultural advancements, to the invention of vaccines, to land and sea exploration. Such skills as information literacy and global awareness are not new, at least not among the elites in different societies" (p. 220).

Brungardt (2011) indicated that as a result of the flattening of the traditional organizational hierarchy, workers at all levels are now required to be proficient in these soft skills. He adds, "as many of these soft skills are required to successfully interact within a collaborative team environment, the possibility of measuring teamwork skills has been explored as a way to measure for soft skill proficiency." Rotherham and Willingham (2010) highlight the existing gap between rhetoric about basic skills and the effective integration of these skills into the formal education framework. "These approaches [skills based learning] are widely acclaimed and can be found in any pedagogical methods text-book; teachers know about them and believe they're effective. And yet, teachers rarely use them."

Today, it is still a challenge for educational institutions (particularly the more conventional ones) to know how to measure, quantify, and qualify these skills. The existence of a gap between rhetoric about skills (e.g., *A nation at risk* report or "Partnership for 21st Century Skills") and the capacity to bring these skills into action (i.e., through multi-contextual learning practices) is still evident. In describing how relevant soft skills have

become, Nickson et al. (2011) added, "the soft skills have become the hard skills."

As Rotherham and Willingham (2010) explain, more than a change in curriculum will be required in order to consistently develop these skills during education and training. Jimenez (2006, p. 72) explains that rather than focusing on rhetoric about skills, the challenge is to promote skills training and their application in different contexts, outside of formal education. He concludes, "teaching such life skills can be integrated into every aspect of the curriculum through discovery-oriented teaching methods that include interactive learning, applying knowledge to real-life problems, integrating teamwork and peer tutoring into the learning process, and inviting student input into the structure and subject matter of lessons" (p. 75). This makes clear why it is extremely important to stimulate the "expert decision making and meta-cognitive strategies that indicate how to proceed when no standard approach seems applicable" (Dede, 2010).

CONCLUSIONS: SHAPING THE KNOWMADIC PROFILE

The future is a complex and constantly transforming challenge. While we might not be able to predict the future, we can still create a future in which we all want to live. If not, we will have to assume the cost of living in an outdated, obsolescent society that neglects the importance of *creating new bridges between the world of education and the fast-paced world of professionals.* This chapter ends with a selection of key ideas that can help to frame the discussion around the various topics that will be significant in the redesign of teaching and learning experiences in the coming years.

1   Interpersonal, social, or soft skills are not exclusive to the 21st century. However, these skills are now fundamental for a broader sector of the population (i.e., not exclusively for the elites as before) as well as for a growing segment of the workforce.

2   Innovations in the education sector have broadly been adopted over the last few decades, particularly when the rhetoric of innovation has been supported by the use of ICTs within the classroom. However, those individuals who are already studying within the formal education system cannot wait for initiatives in educational reform to be implemented. Implementation can take years: too long for those currently in the system. Instead of "educationalizing" all the problems of society, it is probably a better idea to develop personal strategies to learn, unlearn and reskill from different contexts, situations and interactions.

3   Mobility can be (re)considered

as one element that can provide special relevance to students as well as educators. The possibility to learn from other environments and communities, as well as from changing situations, stimulates new combinations of knowledge, disciplines, as well as adaptation and collaboration, among other relevant soft skills. In addition, the creation of new mechanisms to proliferate work-based learning experiences, as well as the adoption of effective feedback from the labor market, should be considered crucial for adjusting formal education to meet the needs of a work-based society.

In exploring a better way to envision the education process for coming generations of students, it would not make sense to ignore the new possibilities, spaces, and tools that we already have at hand. That is why it is important to explore new spaces and chances for learning from new people, disciplines, and expertise. If knowledge is inherently dynamic, it is important to highlight the idea of learning as a life-long journey – a journey which is not limited by any space, institution, or diploma. Keeping in mind the idea of a continuous voyage, Moravec's (2008) concept of the *knowmad* seems to be more than appropriate to describe this expanded learning. He explains:

[A] nomadic knowledge and innovation worker – that is, a creative, imaginative, and innovative person who can work with almost anybody, anytime, and anywhere. Moreover, knowmads are valued for the personal knowledge that they possess, and this knowledge gives them a competitive advantage. Industrial society is giving way to knowledge and innovation work. Whereas the industrialization of Society 1.0 required people to settle in one place to perform a very specific role or function, the jobs associated with knowledge and information workers have become much less specific in regard to task and place. Moreover, technologies allow for these new paradigm workers to work either at a specific place, virtually, or any blended combination. Knowmads can instantly reconfigure and recontextualize their work environments, and greater mobility is creating new opportunities.

Experts, policy makers, educators, and deans – as well as self-trainers, workers, learners, and any individuals interested in the relevance of the development of a multi-skilled profile learners from multi-contextual practices - should explore the usefulness of the *knowmad* concept.

The challenge now, as always, is to bring these ideas to action, and to explore the conditions for triggering those "multi-skilled profiles" which are relevant for stimulating a mode of learning that happens anytime and anywhere. If a knowmad is able to learn and unlearn continuously, then the mismatches described previously will only form part of an endless, but resilient, process of adaptation. It is therefore desirable that the "walled garden" of formal education should find mechanisms and practices to stimulate new forms and nwq modes of learning, encouraging the creation of more suitable education paradigms. At the same time, it is expected that individuals should embrace and share their own strategies to learn continuously.

It is undeniably true that many regions of the world still only value those experiences and knowledge that is supported by a piece of paper or diploma. But it is equally true that the world of work increasingly demands a leveraging of talent through mechanisms that are more flexible. These elements are just symptoms of a much bigger transformation that will happen (*at different speeds*) in the world of education. And, those who suit the knowmad's profile will probably be in a considerably better position to take advantage of these transformations.

REFERENCES

Brungardt, C. 2011. The intersection between soft skill development and leadership education. *Journal of Leadership Education,* *10*(1), 1-21.

Castells, M. (1997). An introduction to the information age. *City,* *2*(7), 6–16.

Cobo, C. (2009). Strategies to promote the development of e-competences in the next generation of professionals: European and International trends. *SKOPE Issues Paper Series.* Retrieved from papers.ssrn.com/sol3/papers.cfm?abstract_id=1904871

Daniels, V. S. (2011). Assessing the value of certification preparation programs in higher education. *American Journal of Business Education* (AJBE), *4*(6), 1–10.

Davies, A., Devin F., and Marina G. (2011). *Future work skills 2020.* Institute for the Future (for the University of Phoenix Research Institute). apolloresearchinstitute.com/sites/default/files/future_work_skills_2020_full_research_report_final_1.pdf

de Bary, B. (2010). *Universities in translation: The mental labor of globalization.* Hong Kong:Hong Kong University Press.

Dede, C. (2010). Comparing frameworks for 21st century skills. In J. Bellanca & R. Brandt (Eds.), *21st century skills: Rethinking how students learn* (pp. 51–76). Bloomington, IN: Solution Tree.

Gardner, D. P. (1983). *A nation at risk: The imperative for educational reform.* Washington, DC: US Government Printing Office. Retrieved from mathcurriculumcenter.org/PDFS/CCM/summaries/NationAtRisk.pdf

Generation Europe Foundation. (2010). *Employing the NEXT Generation 2010: The right skills in the right place at the right time.* Generation Europe Foundation and the FutureWork Forum. Generation Europe Foundation. Retrieved from www.generation-europe.eu/assets/what_we_do/research_and_surveys/GEFWFEmploying-NextGeneration2010final.PDF

George Williams College, & YMCA. (2011). Informal learning. *Infed: the informal education home page and encyclopaedia of informal education.* Retrieved from www. infed.org/

Goleman, D., Boyatziz, R., & McKee, A. (2004). The leadership repertoire. *Primal leadership: Learning to lead with emotional intelligence* (pp. 53 - 69). Boston, MA: Harvard Business School Press.

Hurrell, S. A. (2009). *Soft skills deficits in Scotland: Their patterns, determinants and employer responses.* The University of Strathclyde. Retrieved from ethos. bl.uk/OrderDetails.do?uin=uk. bl.ethos.510680

Jimenez, E. (2006). *World development report 2007: development and the next generation.* World Bank Publications.

Labaree, D. F. (2008). The winning ways of a losing strategy: Educationalizing social problems in the United States. *Educational Theory, 58*(4), 447–460.

Levy, F., & Murnane, R. J. (2004). *The new division of labor: how computers are creating the next job market.* NY: Princeton University Press.

Lindeman, E. C. (1989). The meaning of adult education. A classic North American statement on adult education. ERIC.

McCall, M. W., Lombardo, M. M., & Morrison, A. M. (1988). *The lessons of experience: How successful executives develop on the job.* New York: The Free Press.

Moravec, J. (2008). Toward Society 3.0: A New Paradigm for 21st century education. Presented at the *ASOMEX Technology Conference: Education for Children of the 21st Century,* Monterrey, Mexico.

Nickson, D., Warhurst, C., Commander, J., Hurrell, S. A., & Cullen, A. M. (2012). Soft skills and employability: Evidence from UK retail. *Economic and Industrial Democracy, 33*(1), 65–84.

OECD. (2011). *OECD employment outlook 2011.* Paris: Organisation for Economic Co-operation and Development. Retrieved from www.oecd-ilibrary.org/content/book/empl_outlook-2011-en

Redecker, C., Leis, M., Leendertse, M., Punie, Y., Gijsbers, G., Kirschner, P., Stoyanov, S., et al. (2010). *The future of learning: New ways to learn new skills for future jobs. Results from an online expert consultation.* Seville, Spain: JRC-IPTS.

Rifkin, J. (2010, May 30). Empathic education: The transformation of learning in an interconnected world. *The Chronicle of Higher Education.* Retrieved from chronicle.com/article/Empathic-Education-The/65695/

Rotherham, A. J., & Willingham, D. T. (2010). 21st-century skills: Not new, but a worthy challenge. *American Educator, 34*(1), 17-20.

Shalini, V. (2009). Soft skills for the BPO sector. New Delhi: Pearson Education India.

Shepherd, J. (2011, November 28). Computer lessons are out of date, admits government. *Guardian News.* Retrieved from www. guardian.co.uk/education/2011/nov/28/computer-lessons-out-of-date

Thorndike, R. K. (1920). Intelligence and its uses. *Harper's Magazine,* (140), 227-335.

Tissot, P. (2004). *Terminology of vocational training policy.* European Centre for the Development of Vocational Training. Retrieved from www.biblioteca.porto.ucp. pt/docbweb/MULTIMEDIA/ASSO-CIA/PDF/TERM.PDF

Weinberger, D. (2007.) *Everything is miscellaneous: The power of the New Digital Disorder.* New York: Holt.

Weyand, L. D. (1925). What is industrial education? *American Journal of Sociology, 30*(6), 652-664.

Yu, V. (2010). "Education Futures: An interview with John W. Moravec". The Academy of You. (Interview by Victor Yu.) Retrieved from www. udemy.com/blog/education-futuresjohn-moravec/

notes

Notes

RUIN THIS PAGE!

notes

Learning choreo- graphy

THIEU BESSELINK

'Take ownership of your learning.'

LEARNING IN KNOWMAD SOCIETY IS ABOUT THE EXPERIENCE OF BEING ALIVE AS MUCH AS IT IS ABOUT THE STUDY OF LIFE.

'THE LEARNING CHOREOGRAPHER'S ART IS TO SEE THE INVISIBLE'

THIEU BESSELINK

Learning choreography is creating the conditions for meaningful movement in the development of students and their context.

THE ONLY WAY TO TEACH QUEST EDUCATION IS BY BEING ON A QUEST YOURSELF.

SUMMARY

LEARNING CHOREOGRAPHY
- Thieu Besselink -

This chapter argues we need a *choreography* rather than a curriculum in order to bring reality back into school. I see education in Knowmad Society as a collective work of performance art, the process in which students and teachers are granted a way to find and follow a renewed purpose and relevance of education. What follows is what I call Quest Education, which involves the subjective creation of knowledge and significance in the real world, with the transfer of knowledge, reflection, and experimentation (what we traditionally think of as "education") as supporting elements.

I share insights and experiences my students and I gained by leading the Learning Lab in Amsterdam, and I advocate conscious experimentation that builds the bridge as we walk it:

- Take ownership of your learning.
- Learning in Knowmad Society is about the experience of being alive as much as it is about the study of life.
- Learning for change makers is much less about analysis of the past than it is about designing the future.
- Modern education suffers from abstraction.
- Life and relevance can come back into the learning experience through the urgent quest of the student.
- The only way to teach Quest education is being on a quest yourself.
- Learning choreography is creating the conditions for meaningful movement in the development of students and their context.
- Purposive development starts with a void, not a curriculum.
- Quest Education is not about teaching a subject, but creates the conditions for students to make a difference.
- The learning choreographer's art is to see the invisible.

The modern school, at its best, is a satisfying extension of the unreality of societal perception. As we enter the conclusion of an industrializing age, I recognize that, within its walls, lectures are concerned with an abstract dream of future usefulness, while life is happening between classes. Half of the time, and half asleep, teachers and students keep each other caught in a fiction of relevance: Relevance of knowledge to our lives, relevance of the relationships to each other, and relevance to the questions of our time and to the society in which we live.

At its birth, however, the modern school emancipated millions of people out of dependency. By the start of this millennium, schooling has elevated more people out of poverty and ignorance than anything else in history using the same principles of efficiency that underlie the industrial age.

Just as the modern school of the 20th century knew its *raison d'être* and the role it requires of its teachers, schools in Knowmad Society need to find their place and purpose in the society they create. We know schools shape society, which, in my mind, is what education ought to be focused on. They are a primary force of personal and social change. If that is so, what is the role of teaching? Or, more specifically, how do we teach *purposively* for social change?

Imagine that we are staging a performance that intends to participate in the creation of our collective narrative. A dance or theatre piece that is not made simply for its own sake, but is designed to have an impact and contribute to the understanding of ourselves and the world in which we live. Video artists, soundscapers, actors, stage designers, dancers, costume makers, the director, and even the audience all participate from their perspective roles. It is an endeavor to create a work of art that supersedes each individual. Theater makers and performers know that in order to create something that matters, something that responds to an urgent and higher need of fulfillment, they will have to learn and change as they go along, and that their learning and changing is part of the art that they create. The performance piece thereby becomes a vehicle through which each person can develop and express him- or herself; and, in this state of interdependency, the group collectively evolves to make a mark. No director would merely impose a play for this to happen, but rather guide the collective process.

I see education for knowmads as such: a collective work of performance art. The action research I do for this type of education is always about looking for the kind of learning, type of structure, and appropriate interventions that actively gives form to new resilient and meaningful relationships, because it is in the nature of relationships that new societies are made.

The metaphor of choreography and directing here is not classical, but it is an approach that I have in common with the way philosopher Christopher Alexander (1979) sees architecture and urban development in *The timeless way of building*, or with the way Falk Richter creates and directs his performances. Born in Hamburg, Germany, in 1969, Richter is a theatre maker and director. Among his works are *Gott ist ein DJ*, *Electronic city*, *Protect me*, and *Trust*. In his works, text and movement flow in and out of an emerging narrative. This is true with respect to the experience of the audience, but perhaps even more so for the performers themselves, who, during the process of creation, are discovering what the piece could be as they are building it. Patterns emerge from concentrated work. What fascinates me is that, here, learning is a form of making and creating a form of learning.

In this essay, I share some of the building blocks of this creational learning process that I discovered during the research at The Learning Lab, which is a think-tank for social change. The action research I am referring to in this chapter has mainly taken place at the University of Amsterdam with four cohorts of honors students across various disciplines and nationalities. See www.thelearninglab.nl for more details.

THE QUEST

I write from a place and time where I see education struggling with its place in society. I often encounter a search for meaning and direction when I help schools or universities in their transition. At the same time, I see many students and teachers struggle with the place of education in their lives. An "education" and its forms and procedures are simply taken for granted. Modern education's objectives of emancipation and industrialization have been accomplished, and innovation in education occurs only under strict and conservative inspection. All of the above leads schools and their constitu-ent participants to search for their story in the minor margins of freedom they still have – in small moments of aliveness between teacher and student, for instance, or the relatively unregulated space between classes.

We no longer live within the needs of an industrial society. We have moved up the hierarchy of Maslow (1943) it seems. This means that our needs and values shifted from material safety toward a need for higher-order learning: significance and self-actualization (see also Inglehart, 1990). This refers to the felt need to be creative as human beings and to actualize becoming the best "version" of ourselves.

It is no coincidence that both the institution of education and the students are on a quest to find their assignment. The context within which I speak about learning is therefore that of a *quest*, rather than a transfer of knowledge. It is a creative practice, and a creative inquiry. The aim of which always goes beyond the abstract goals of learning as preparation, and instead follows a definite higher purpose for which qualitative learning today is required to address and fulfill. I am not denying the need for knowledge transfer, but we have a lot of that already –and its methods are becoming ever more advanced with the rise of the digital age.

I am writing for the change makers that do not see their job as merely a means to make a living, but as a vehicle for the creative expression of their gift to society. Creativity is on everyone's agenda, but the way I use it here is not for the generation of good ideas. It instead refers to the conscious "world making," i.e., participating with one's surroundings, exercising one's character, and employing one's enthusiasms. In short: putting their passion and agency into action. I am not talking about how to teach geography, for example, but share my experiences in helping geographers become self-directed change agents in their field. I hope, however, that content-oriented teachers take away some of the principles, and work what inspired them into an attitude or approach that makes their learning environments more "real."

This essay is, in particular, for the people who educate the system hackers of our world. "Hackers," as I use the word, are the people who are able to move a system with elegant interventions. They know it better than anyone, and know how to avoid its constraining structures. They put themselves at stake by standing up against the community in service of the community.

In the Lab, students ask themselves what really matters to themselves in their "world." A quest is born. An econometrics student asks why there is so little critical internal dialogue and fundamental research within his discipline. How can the econometrics that helped design the fatal financial models for the capital crisis of 2008 become self-aware and discover its responsibility. He decided he wanted to show the unreliable and purposefully obscuring foundations of his discipline. He put himself on the line for the sake of living a life in line with the person he wanted to be. Another student searches for a way to make a dance performance for which she can be simultaneously thoroughly prepared and be able to follow urgent inspiration of what emerges from her own creation. This was a very conscious project inspired by her quest to redefine her personal relationship with the world and the origin of human creativity. A quest could also be the desire of a group of students to set up a hydrogen taxi service from Schiphol Airport as not only a way to set an example, but also connect key players in society from different fields around a root issue of our exhaustive (energy) economy. It is, for students, a profound experience to wake up to the possibility that they can find and follow their quest.

In education as a quest, the question educators need to ask is not what students should learn, but how to create the conditions for movement to become meaningful. This encompasses the knowledge, opinions, and skills to join the will to create and turn them into a craft that can be extend to their communities. The quest is the domain of *homo faber*, the creating human being, who creates "his" world and the meaning he finds in it.

The need for *The Quest* is not particular to education; it is an intrinsic part of life. However, what is particular to the education I am writing about here, is the focused time of a diverse group of people in a contained space that is designed for the possibility of development in reality, including questions, actions, encounters, and decisions to become real matters of life and inner death. This is what makes The Quest so exciting, dangerous, and beautiful.

Who remembers what he or she learned in school or university? That we turned out reasonably well is a sign that it wasn't so much the content we retained or the skills we acquired, but rather a reflection of the quest we pursued that made the difference. Perhaps most schools work despite themselves, and provide a legitimate hangout for a searching youth. My initial thought when I started to design learning environments for universities was, "why not feature the hangout in education?"

THE VOID

The hangout we created at The Learning Lab was The Void, but it was not empty. What Richter and Alexander have in common is that they both start from a void in which everyone involved can enter with his or her history, aspirations, inspirations, needs, and get to work. It starts with emptying out and "unlearning," if you like, the presets that students come with. They can no longer play the role of student and have to become humans with real questions. Filling the space with these questions includes the relationships they have with what is happening in the world around them as well as the ties they have with people and places outside the room. The time and circumstances dictate the urgency and direction of "building" (Alexander, 1979). For us at the Lab, it meant that The Void was being filled with material that we the "students" and "teachers" brought in. The material we brought in was then in the form of circumstances that were important to us (i.e., news articles, scientific findings, movies, personal stories). And, we brought in our dreams, fears, and dispositions. They would all determine the direction of learning in the Lab. This is the first condition I found for learning to be alive. Like architecture or performance, learning needs to relate intimately to the questions asked by the learner.

Consequently, the time we share is about how we fill The Void with what everyone does with his or her time, and what each of us wants to emerge from our combined intentions, hopes, fears, interests, and capacities. We usually start in a place that sets the stage and context for this particular quest. In those first days, we try to find out why we are together. Though, sometimes at the end of the Lab, we serendipitously find out that where we ended up is somewhere completely different than what we thought we "signed up for." But that is the nature of a quest. You also find what you were not looking for, and would have never found had you just planned a route from point A to point B.

In The Void, we suddenly realize that we are not "students," but are instead people with a history and a perspective. While on The Quest, and by filling The Void, The Learning Lab becomes a choreography. This is not in the sense of "time writing" (choreography) where time and space are sculpted with bodies (much like a curriculum predefines the time and space in school), but in the sense of sculpting scripts and patterns that map the coordinates for movement, not the movement itself.

Contemporary choreographic questions fueling the performance of today are typically:

- What do we really (want to) know for this project?
- What do we really want to change?
- What would we really want to make?
- How do we really want to work?
- Who do we really want to be?
- What should be built?
- What should be researched?

SEIZING THE MOMENT

I came to believe that the kind of learning I am looking for is always asserted in the present moment, and that the questions we explore need to be "hot" in the here and now. That means we have to deal with the world in the midst of change, and we have to deal with learners at a level and phase for which they are ready. Learning, from this perspective, consists of all those things for which you cannot prepare, just as the practice of teaching consists of all those things for which you cannot prepare. It is this alertness to what reality "is" that can make education more real than day-to-day life, rather than a simulation or preparation "for" life. This is also what makes it difficult to describe, teach, or accept, because it can be disturbing, unpredictable, and elusive.

For instance, a student looks back with disappointment on his failure to realize the film he wanted to make at the Lab. But, by taking that disappointment as material with which to explore the key moments of development for him, he can discover that the result was less important than the journey he took, because it had been a courageous one. This is a classic moment, but it is still impossible to prepare a class that deals with this theme because it loses its relevance the moment it is not connected to the experience being had.

Of course, there is a preparation of the conditions for learning to emerge, and there is a lot of preparation of the teacher's capacities to design learning environments or an ability to intervene in the process of learning in appropriate ways. Building one's alertness is probably the biggest challenge for knowmad teachers. I would say it takes more time and effort than giving a series of lectures. But, the moment of learning, the pedagogical moment, comes unexpectedly, and has to be seized in the moment.

MAKING SENSE

In a knowmadic society, significance is not a given, and much less socially shared. Whereas we used to find common purpose in grand narratives of progress or religion, a post-modern wave of fragmentation has given us the opportunity to find new coherence in the individual stories we live and in the dispersed narratives we collectively build. Learning in a knowmad society therefore involves developing the capacity to take ownership over one's own development, and the ability to give a fulfilling meaning to one's experiences.

In education, the origin of this senselessness lies partly in our collective migration away from relevance and towards ab-straction. Dewey (1929) famously warned for the "intellectual fallacy" that led Western culture to value abstraction more real than the particular and concrete. Only what is thinkable or can be put into words is real. Affections, values, intuitions and volitions are excluded from the real world and delegated to the "personal" realm in favor of abstract knowledge. What matters to us as individuals has had little or no place in schooling, which explains why schools never paid attention to how to develop in students a good sense of what matters to them.

Also, learning for obsolete, others', and abstract standards that have very little to do with us is a major cause for root-lessness. Rootlessness is the condition describing discon-nectedness from what matters most to us, and to which we cannot find a meaningful relationship. In school, the things we are asked to memorize, analyze, or creatively reproduce no longer connect us to our futures, as they used to do when an education was a highly-valued path to a highly-valued job within industrial society. But, to connect, you need to have a sense of who you are. Society forces us to be free in choosing who we want to be by challenging every answer we find for ourselves with the possibility of an alternative identity. Only by providing conditions for personal significance to arise, we move beyond a postmodern education of deconstruction.

Why we need choreography rather than a curriculum becomes clear when you realize that, as Søren Kierkegaard is attributed to have said in various ways throughout his career, "life is forwardly lived, and backwardly understood." Learning for change makers is much less about analysis of the past than it is about designing the future. However, since no one knows the future, especially in times of fundamental systems change, we make sense of our experiences when we look back or as we go along. Artists use applied theory or methods of hypothesis testing only for their technical development, but the significance and understanding of the work comes in reverse order. First, you do something, then meaning is constructed. It would also imply a reversal of the curriculum in this respect. In the past, students would follow a prescribed curriculum, now the "curriculum" follows the student. Naturally, the meaning of what a curriculum "is" changes with it. This suggests a complete reversal of the way we think about learning. The choreographer is, first and foremost, an agent in sense-making.

In complex, unknowable environments that change rapidly, and where, for instance, even big companies do not give the security of a career as they may fall almost as quickly as a startup stands, having your own compass straight is the only thing that keeps you on a path that makes sense. Keeping ownership over your life requires something entirely different than it did some decennia ago. Feelings of ownership and self-direction used to come with a reliable job and possessing a particular expertise, but jobs and expertise change too often today to give your control. It becomes more difficult to tell a coherent story of who you are or what you are here for when your occupation changes so rapidly as it does today. This is what I learned from my mentor Richard Sennett, who described the loss of this personal coherency in his book, *The corrosion of character* (Sennett, 1998). For Sennett, the most vulnerable people in society are left to the whims of a perverted capitalism, and so he resists the culture of flexibility. And, whereas I also think that the form of capitalism we created poses us with this problem, I believe our best way out is through flexibility because it is part of the paradigm that we are adapting to.

Schools, alone, cannot give students the conditions for a fulfilling life, and especially not to the most vulnerable groups in society. Not everyone is nor can be a knowmad, if by that, we mean someone who can deal with fundamental uncertainty. We will have to develop new socioeconomic relationships that offer new kinds of security for the vast majority of society. This requires the art of becoming comfortable with being on a never-ending quest and choosing new dependencies that can help us deal with the uncertainties inherent in a knowmad society. A continuous learning experience, with no clear destination, but stronger and more meaningful social bonds, is related to the creation of significance that lies at the heart of learning.

All of a sudden, the relationships students built with one another and the people they met in their projects became part of their journey, and featured in the road maps they made to look back at what and how they learned. Knowing your dependencies gives you the power to turn them into relationships of reciprocity and recognition that strengthen you on your path of personal reinvention. Also looking back and becoming skillful storytellers allowed them to "connect the dots" as Steve Jobs spoke of at his commencement speech at Stanford, of their chaotic and discontinuous lives, and form a new coherence (Stanford University, 2005).

Moving from a philosophy of *knowledge* to a philosophy of the *purposive experience of meaning* means letting go of the idea that the most important thing in school is learning theories and practices that later, in real life, have to be applied. This sounds radical and so far from what we are familiar with that we may be tempted to think that it implies we would not learn skills and facts anymore. This is not what it implies, however. It only suggests we should connect knowledge and skills together to construct meaningful experiences.

When talking about specific knowledge and skills, in the beginning I thought we had to cover a lot of material, understand many concepts by dealing with them, but I discovered that the actual knowledge development comes when one idea is followed all the way down in all of its dimensions: personal, social, objective, subjective, etc. This is all needed in order to come to the essence of what the teacher/choreographer and the students are learning. It would be a great mistake, however, to take this search for "the essence" as a form of specialization. The point is not to study more divisions of the same thing, getting deeper into one facet of an idea, but it is discovering the relationships of the parts to the whole. Understanding these relationships exceeds one's knowledge of the particular artifact, and makes it transferable to other domains. It assures that whatever it is we are studying makes sense on more than one level of understanding.

THE CONTEXT

Before discussing more about the choreographer, I'd like to explore the context of this teaching form. If we divide types of learning experiences between consuming and creating experiences on one hand, and in objective and subjective experiences on the other, we can easily say from our own experiences how most teaching takes place as transfer of known knowledge, as a reflection of how the student is doing, or as an experiment, or as problem-based learning. But, unless the problems arise from a felt need in the learner, or the knowledge transferred was specifically asked for, there is only very little learning going on, much less development. All knowledge is subjective in the sense that it is always known and valued by a person.

The challenge in a knowmad society will be to find ways in assisting the creation of *subjective knowledge* that gives relevance to objective facts observed, the information downloaded, and what was experienced. Transfer is what a teacher, book or website conveys to the learner. The experiment is concerned with an event that can be measured and experienced, and reflection is generally the perspective a teacher can give concerning the performance of the learner. In this scheme, a created, subjective knowledge follows from a quest, and it is this quest, with a definite path and purpose, which weaves the other three learning modes into a coherent whole.

Figure 3. The learning quadrant

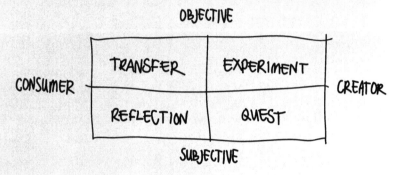

THE WORK

If we let go of the idea of a fixed curriculum as a program carefully designed by the genius of the teacher, and instead imagine a set of simple rules that define the playing field through which the building blocks of an urgent learning journey are gathered by its knowmads, then teaching becomes the mastery of process and the creative direction of the adventure. The adventure spins a new lexicon of understanding, every time again, and can never be the same nor follow the same path.

Our language, however, often keeps us from thinking beyond the patterns that we know. If we do not understand the importance of adventure, it is because we confuse it with entertainment. If we fail to understand initiation, it is because we think of distant tribes. If we do not get the meaning of a quest, it is because we lost touch with our need for truth-seeking rather than fact finding. If we believe beauty has no place in learning, it is because we mistake it for embellishment. And, if educators do not see love as the quintessence of education, it is because we think of it as romance. Learning for change makers means finding a new language, time after time, through an aesthetic experience that is so convincing that our beliefs about what we thought substantial become changeable.

In my research for the kind of process design that can contain a knowmad's learning journey, I have tried to stay away from fixed methods, and instead tried to reinvent forms and language for every new situation. Even though it was tempting to reuse methods, or use a great method simply because I thought it was interesting (a very difficult one to suppress), the trick was to stay with THE question. THE question was either, "what do they really need me for now," or "what am I doing?" "Am I trying to convince anyone?" "Am I really helping?" "Am I listening?" And, so on.

The matter was too complex to know in advance what needed to be done. Together with the people with whom I worked, we had to act fast, and, as I often say, "in the moment." The foundation on which those actions were based was on the accumulated experience that we had with experiential learning, a good general training, dedicated reflected practice of past situations, and our intuition.

I found that a successful learning journey is one in which personal and group purpose lead to manifest value, and leans heavily on the "choreographer's" ability to observe the relationships that really matter. There are countless parameters when dealing with a co-creative group dynamic, and knowing which ones do the work at a given moment turned out crucial. That means not getting bogged down in the details, but keeping key purpose and our process in mind at all times. Otherwise, you run the risk of asking things of your students that they are not ready for, for which there is no context yet, or it makes students lose sight of the bigger picture. The craft was in the observations of what makes movement, what provokes learning, and what causes the will of the learner to engage. Sometimes this means not telling what the larger context is of where you want to go as a choreographer, as it may be too overwhelming or abstract and take focus away of what is relevant now for the learners. It is providing a guiding hand by which you discover the territory together.

The Learning Lab was intended to be as much as a laboratory for me as it was for the students. I was setting myself up for failure, but this was necessary to cultivate a clear sense of judgment. What I discovered was that the very condition of being in an experiment together enabled a special kind of learning, and a form of excitement that could not be created otherwise. In this, I refer to the kind of learning where you not only studying a subject, but also yourself. The way you learn becomes part of the study. In this regard, the research method became the "teaching" method!

Even though I may often begin from a void, designing a lab or learning quest is not completely free of structure. It is also not just a series of experiments put together. Without the boundaries of an assignment (whether self-imposed or not) there is no medium for the learning, in the same way that bedding forms a medium that allows water to flow and become a river. The other way around is also true, that without the purpose and passion of the choreographer and learner, there is nothing to grow in the medium, and nothing to flow within the bedding.

Every attempt at designing the entire experience runs into trouble, as the predictions made about what will be needed at a certain moment are invariably wrong. The program changes all the time, according to the actual needs and activities taking place. There is no perfect design, and no design is ever finished. "Everything is always in *beta*," as my students used to say. To adjust and repair the program is therefore not a sign of failure, but a desired part of the process in which we ensure that we are always learning and stay true to the needs and urgency of the group.

THE CHOREOGRAPHER

When a group of learners gathers for the first time, it is always exciting. Many questions, doubts, and unspoken expectations fill the space and all eyes are focused on the "teacher." In the philosophy of many education reformers today, the teacher's task is to adjust his program to the students' needs, as a coach without content. But, I found a very important qualification to that desire during the research. Coaching is too passive in my view, and limits itself to the development of the learner and his or her acquisition of knowledge and skills. A choreographer, by contrast, is also staging a piece. Closer to the university system, I would compare it with the scientist who builds his research with his students. I found that I was on a mission as much as they were, even if mine included finding ways to tease out theirs. Again, my capacity was not as a "teacher," but as creator of a reality, the transformation of higher education, and the process of which I used to design learning experiences for "students." What, in my case, emerged as an innovation in education as such could well be another teacher's change in healthcare, or teaching English to immigrants from the community.

In my conversations with Falk Richter, I discovered how much of this role is akin to that of the director. The word "director" gives an indication of how substantial his role could be in co-designing and guiding the architecture of a learning quest. A teacher as director gains the freedom to follow his creative capacity. When framed in by imposed curricula, the teacher can only try to create his freedom. But, if we are to educate change makers, then teachers should be change makers, and be an example of what is possible in both character and capacity. The only way to develop these is by stepping up and beginning the exploration. Moreover, if the teacher is not learning, himself, he is not transferring the experience of learning.

A teacher can start with a vision of what he wants to see in the world. But, working from the void, this vision is shaped and made concrete by the material that the students bring in. The director or choreographer looks for a certain quality in the building blocks from which the journey is made –particularly that of a certain aliveness. His sense of quality depends on his own aesthetic capacity. A creative choreographer needs to reinvent himself every time, or as much as is necessary to be able to be truly interested in what he is doing. It is not enough to just do your thing. It may suffice for the transfer of knowledge, but it will not help knowmads navigate the chaos inherent in modern society. He needs to research himself all the time in order to know what he is looking for in the group of learners, what he wants to make with them, and what they want to create with him. His art is to see the invisible, as Michelangelo famously saw a finished sculpture from a block of marble. That is true for a whole quest, but also for every moment or person. He is good at seeing possibilities for development and interesting paths as they arise in the moment. These possibilities are where life resides. Something lacks life, or relevance when, as I said, if a question or action does not arrive from an actual urgency.

Over the course of the Lab, students slowly appropriate the space and will try out how far they can go. The "dance" develops under the gaze of the choreographer. In many ways, this dance is what Wittgenstein (1953) would call a "language game." This is spontaneous and moves in flux, but, at the same time, is governed by rules developed during the performance from which the dance derives its meaning.

By becoming part of the performance, the choreographer senses what is appropriate, mis-, dis-, un-, or inappropriate for this space. There are borders that the choreographer sets and on their quest students feel out where they are. The coordinating, enabling, and sometimes subversive role of the learning choreographer is that of an indirect and implicit filter. If one is too explicit about why something falls outside of the scope of appropriateness, students will close off vast fields of possibilities and creativity just to fulfill their idea of your expectation of them. Give too little, and they cannot commit fully to your guidance. Sometimes the guidance meets with resistance because it violates the identities of the students, or their concept of what quest they are on. This violence is essential for the learning process. This is why I mirror the emergent protocol for the lab in a subversive way. The dance holds direction, but fundamentally stays the work of and keeps the identity of the performers. Students call it magic sometimes, because they have a continuous feeling of not knowing the entire picture while they do feel I have a sense of the possibilities and quality for their work in any particular time and space.

This is the subtle matter that the choreographer has to deal with in order for the learning to generate itself and for a meaningful movement to emerge from frictions and collaboration amongst the students and between the desires and (im)possibilities of they encounter.

The role of the choreographer is then the assistance in selecting engaging material with which the group can build upon, to tease out experiences, tap into sources of inspiration, and help compose the energy that will be the building blocks for The Quest.

Possibilities for real learning and purposive creation are those possibilities that call up people's desires to make conscious decisions, that wake them up, and make them present-minded. They are possibilities for truth. The choreographer invites truth, which is never a consumed fact but a created reality, by first seeing what narratives wants to emerge from the group or the student, and then teasing it out with an intervention. Interventions can be anything ranging from a simple question to assignments, disrupting or contributing actions, stories, or large scale operations that set a context or process. Next to the context and relationships, interventions are the main instrument of the learning choreographer. Interventions need to be systemic. That is, they need to be aimed at those acupuncture points in the living organism or "ecology" of the student that will take away what blocks development. In the same way that it takes a village to raise a child, it takes an ecology of ideas and experiences to develop a student. In education for a knowmad society, it is crucial that students are not just subject to this ecology, but they need to understand their place within the ecology and be able to act within it. The community, sources of knowledge and experience, mentorship, supportive infrastructure, social and historical context, network, situational potential, all play part in the learning ecology. I will elaborate a little further, below.

PEDAGOGY OF RESISTANCE

In English, the word "pedagogy" seldom bares the Dutch meaning of *pedagogie*, or the German *Bilding* or *Erziehung*. What they point at is not a form of instruction, but the responsibility teachers take for the process by which students become a fully-developed human beings, engaged with the reality of the world. For practical reasons, however, allow me to use the word "pedagogy" here.

The interventions of the choreographer are pedagogical, and they are usually not a very comfortable set of interventions. Because taking away blockages to development are not about smoothing out the road, but often are quite the opposite. They try to organize a dialogue between the learner and the world because the main question that underlies all processes that I described in this chapter is *whether you are willing to be alive or not*. The principal pedagogical aim of the choreographer is to create the experience of what it means to be alive in this world. This experience challenges the prejudices, beliefs, and fantasies to which we tend to retreat in order not to feel the challenges that life poses to our being. If we accept the challenge, then we would have to change ourselves, but it would also mean that the beliefs and identity that we invested in so much are going down the drain. If we do not retreat into denial, we might attack and destroy the ideas, people, or things that challenge the comfortable images we have of ourselves. It takes courage, attentiveness, and persistence to bare the resistance of life. And, it is in that space of resistance that we truly learn, where we discover the other side of what was hidden until that moment. Taking away a block to learning means taking away the flight or fight response. To prevent over-simplistic thinking or fundamentalism, it means doing whatever it takes to keep people from fooling themselves, hiding from reality, or destroying that reality.

In a movie that was made about The Learning Lab, you can see students meeting each other for the first time at a graveyard at night to experience and reflect on what they really want to do with the time they have, both in their lives and in the Lab (see the film by van Doorn & Smit, 2010). The most uncomfortable part of that experience was not the graveyard, but the fact that they had no assignment to guide them. They were simply sent out with flashlights. In the absence of clear expectations from the teacher, it came down to the students, themselves, to decide what this could mean for them, and how they would use their time. After the initial giggling and holding on to each other, the learning stage became silent and questions would start to come up in their minds. They were different for everyone, but they had something to do with the question, "what am I doing?" This is a very confrontational question if you take it to its fullest consequences. This experience prepared the ground for deep learning in the months that would follow by opening up an attentiveness to one's own behavior and thoughts, and the awareness that each of us is responsible for his or her own reality and initiative.

THE LEARNING ECOLOGY

As the development of change makers is as much about making as it is about forming theories, and about personal growth as it is about collective creation, an environment in which this can all happen is necessarily a rich, integrated, multi-layered whole, which I see more as an ecosystem in which students grow than a delineated course that they take.

The more we recognize the diversity in ways that people develop themselves, the less obvious it becomes that a random group of learners is thrown in a room with the teacher who happened to teach a certain subject. The less obvious also it is that there is one kind of schooling, hence the "ecologies of learning" that Moravec (in Cobo & Moravec, 2011) refers to. How these people find each other will become more important as more universities start using related practices. The reason is that students and teachers need to be able to commit their biographies to the development of personal purpose.

The learning ecology I talk about revolves, in a micro scale, around the Lab, and a very important part of it involved the people guiding the Lab. A large part in directing a creative inquiry is the assembly of the right team, and this includes the learning agents as well as the students. The right team is that group of people which can build up a context and energy strong enough to support the insecurities, questions, and aspirations of the students. The chemistry of the group is incredibly important. Whereas teachers are normally simply allocated according to the subjects they teach, we will have to look for new partnerships that support the needs of the learning team.

During the Lab, I experienced taking many different, sometimes conflicting roles, each responsible for an aspect of the internal learning ecology. Some can be united in one person, others would probably be best divided up between a team of learning agents, sometimes also including students. In the Lab we conducted in 2011, my students developed a series of ideal types that can help us understand the ecology of the creative inquiry that a quest consists of. Here are a few examples:

- The "unlearner" is the agent I most intensely use at the beginning of every quest. He helps students re-frame their realities and become free of their habitual patterns of thinking and observing. There is no predetermined method, which makes it a difficult role to fulfill. I tend to compare it to the "trickster" in mythology, who we recognize by his unconventional behavior. He breaks the normal rules and expectations and shows us that the world is not what we think it is, and that we are not who we think we are. He may give an idea about what may also be possible, beyond what we hitherto thought.
- The "collective intelligence cultivator" is the agent that makes sure that the knowledge and experiences that are scattered over the learning community are shared and that the group can build on it.
- The "Zeitgeist capturer" places learning journeys in the context of current paradigms. He connects people and initiatives to contemporary trends, or arranges the conditions under which awareness of the emergent realities of the Zeitgeist can arise.

- The "social capital connector" takes care of the relationships and dynamics of social value creation in the community. If we want to learn and create beyond what any individual is capable of by him- or herself, the social capital of the group needs to grow incredibly strong. It may take unconventional methods to make it come forth, and there is no prescribed, mechanical procedure to follow that leads a group to develop it. Hence, it possesses a specific role in the learning ecology.
- The "meaning miner" facilitates the process of meaning making and the creation of a shared language of the learning experiences. This may be the most important task of the learning agents as it is here where the knowledge is made rather than downloaded. It is also something that students cannot naturally do by themselves as the quality of significance gained depends on the awareness, depth and connectedness of the context to which the personal experiences are related. When following the idea of a life forwardly lived, and backwardly understood, the meaning comes after the experience. Industrial education believes meaning comes pre-fabricated and can be applied to a future context, whereas knowmadic education encounters unknown situations that have to be made sense of all the time.
- The "assesmentor" designs and helps design the way learning is measured and evaluated as a form of feedback that gives insight into one's growth rather than a test for judgment. When learning pathways become personalized, and follow an unpredictable path on which new knowledge is created, assessment needs to be co-designed.

Together with the student, the assesmentor determines on what terms and parameters, and in what ways measurement takes place.

CONCLUSION

Teaching in the Knowmad Society is not a regular teaching job. It is a call to bring reality back into learning. The Quest is one way. What I believe will be of profound influence on the practice of learning and schooling is the encounter with an unpredictable path. It takes a knowmad to guide one on that path. The less certainty we have about the externalities of life, which inevitably comes with a globalizing world, the more certainly we need to be able to trust on our internal lives. I believe that a pedagogy of resistance is essential is developing that trust, which means that teaching will entail a substantially larger role for Bildung. Not just Bildung expressed as cultural or intellectual self-cultivation, as Von Humboldt intended it, but also as a practical and creative engagement with the world in which students actively shape.

Orchestrating this dialogue with a not-yet-sustainable world is what teaching in a knowmad society should be about if it is to be an inhabitable society at all. The purpose of this education would be both the development of resilient futures, as well as learning to create new meaning. The ability to personally and collectively make sense and give meaning to life has become much more important at the end of the industrial era where everything can mean anything and everyone can become anyone. Creating relevance, in other words, is the major challenge. At the same time, a part of our path is dictated by the developments in the world, its changing economy, social and cultural make up, and an exhausted ecology. Much of what is relevant is determined by the need to redesign the systems in which we live, and the clues for which will emerge from a sincere engagement with these systems.

Learning choreography is thus not about teaching a subject, but creates the conditions for students to make a difference, whether they are chemists, economists, engineers, or advertising agents. It takes more than a curriculum to do that. Above all, it takes more than a teacher. It requires someone who can guide the pursuit for relevance and meaning through the necessary developments of personal capacity. This takes teaching far beyond any particular subject, and extends into whatever it takes to assist the student to find freedom and purpose in his or her personal and collective aspirations.

CODA

I want to thank our students who worked on the learning ecology, in particular: Arik Beremzon, Eva van Barneveld, Helene Damm, Iona van Dijk, Lisa Gondalatch, Maaike Boumans, Maarten van Schie, Max Geueke, Moos Hueting, Philo van Kemenade, Siri Lijfering, Vitanis Susiskas, and Zinzi Wits. I also want to thank Jack Gallegher, Falk Richter, Betul Ellialtioglu, and Gerard van de Ree for the inspiring conversations that helped shape my work and thoughts.

REFERENCES

Alexander, C. (1979). *The timeless way of building.* New York: Oxford University Press.

Cobo, C., & Moravec, J. W. (2011). *Aprendizaje invisible: Hacia una nueva ecología de la educación.* Barcelona: Laboratori de Mitjans Interactius / Publicacions i Edicions de la Universitat de Barcelona.

Dewey, J. (1929). *Experience and nature.* New York: Dover.

van Doorn, V., & Smit, J. (Writers). (2010). The pioneers lab. Retrieved from www.thelearninglab.nl

Inglehart, R. (1990). *Culture shift in advanced industrial society.* Princeton, N.J.: Princeton University Press.

Maslow, A. H. (1943). A theory of human motivation. *Psychological Review, 50*(4), 370-396.

Sennett, R. (1998). *The corrosion of character: The personal consequences of work in the new capitalism.* New York: Norton.

Stanford University. (2005, June 14, 2005). Text of Steve Jobs' commencement address, *Stanford News.*

Wittgenstein, L. (1953). *Philosophical investigations.* Blackwell.

notes

notes

notes

notes

notes

Sudbury schools and democratic education in Knowmad Society

CHRISTEL HARTKAMP

'It is a misconception that learning equals knowledge. It is the process of learning that makes a person knowledgeable.'

'THE CONCEPT OF "INTELLECTUALITY" HAS DEVELOPED OVER TIME INTO A SYNONYM FOR "BOOK WISDOM," STEERED BY THE KNOWLEDGE BESTOWED BY A CURRICULUM.'

'EDUCATION IS MORE THAN SCHOOLING.'

CHRISTEL HARTKAMP

'THE PARADOX IS, WE ARE ALL PRODUCTS OF A TRADITIONAL SCHOOLING SYSTEM, AND WE ARE TASKED WITH TRYING TO DESIGN FUTURE-RELEVANT EDUCATION.'

"WE CAN'T SOLVE PROBLEMS BY USING THE SAME KIND OF THINKING WE USED WHEN WE CREATED THEM."
Albert Einstein

SUMMARY

**SUDBURY SCHOOLS AND
DEMOCRATIC EDUCATION
IN KNOWMAD SOCIETY**
- Christel Hartkamp -

Skills needed for a future enveloped in rapid change and ambiguity include: creativity, flexibility, and open-mindedness. This requires students that are naturally curious, not afraid to make mistakes, and intelligent in ways to quickly learn new knowledge and skills. What approaches to education can best develop these students? In other words, how can we support a child best to adapt to perceived chaos and uncertainty of the unknown, and be successful? We are reinforcing old paradigms of learning in a changing world. The system, itself, is outdated, and more kids are suffering, both physically or by being labeled and over-cared for. As a result, student motivation is decreasing. The time is ripe to develop real alternatives to the mainstream model.

In our journey to find alternative approaches to education for our daughter, my husband and I were introduced to democratic education, and, in particular, Sudbury model schools. Democratic schools are designed around the concept that children come into the world explicitly designed to educate themselves through their self-directed play and exploration. These schools recognize that kids are vibrant, energetic, interested, motivated, self-aware and naturally inclined to learn – and that the learning does not need to be dictated by external actors.

Democratic schools, and more specifically, Sudbury schools, are believed to support development of skills that are essential in Knowmad Society. These schools are designed around freedom and responsibility. In Sudbury schools, the responsibility is real. Children grow up as self-starters, showing initiative and entrepreneurialism, knowing how to use knowledge, their talents, and how to make decisions on the basis of their own judgments. They know how to steer their lives with the guidance of their own inner compass, and make use of all resources needed to fulfill their goals.

WHAT FORM OF EDUCATION PREPARES YOUTH FOR KNOWMAD SOCIETY?
>>

In 2001, my husband Peter and I started a journey in search of alternative approaches to formal education. Our oldest daughter had serious trouble with learning in the traditional school system; she was demotivated and depressed by the age of eight. The teachers wanted us to believe that there was a problem with her, but we could not agree. We were sure that it had nothing to do with her innate learning skills. We were certain that it all had to do with the way she was forced to learn. We had her tested for "gifted under-achievement," and at the same time, I researched literature on motivation and underachievement in schools.

By studying these articles, we realized that in a traditional school, even in a Waldorf or Montessori school, the development of talents and capabilities of a child depends on so many factors that are not child-related. Metaphorically speaking, this is like placing your child in a big, black box. No matter the innate capabilities and talents, what comes out of the box after so many years is molded by numerous influences. Most of those factors are externally-driven that are hard to influence by the child him- or herself. Influencing factors include feeling comfortable with yourself, the influence of friends, the development of your brain, the expectations of the teacher, and the climate of the school (Jolles, 2012).

My husband, who works as a business consultant, linked these ideas with motivational factors in work. True motivation has to do with what people want to achieve; what they really want for themselves. Exercising and building up pressure do not motivate people. They should be attracted by their own internal needs and desires (see esp. Pink, 2009). So, in our view, what is right for adults in organizations is also right for children in schools. Ryan and Deci (2000) described, with their theory of self-determination, the contextual factors to facilitate healthy psychological development, namely: competence, autonomy, and relatedness. Provided all three factors are met, this should lead to increased self-motivation, optimal growth, and psychological healthiness. Our daughter showed us so clearly that she needed autonomy, and that she needed to feel competent, understood, and accepted.

In an Internet search for resources and ideas, we came across the website of the Sudbury Valley School in Massachusetts. I remember the first time I visited their site: I really found it awkward. I could not imagine a place where kids were left free to develop themselves. It took some time before I started reading more about their philosophy of independence.

The fundamental premises of the school are simple: that all people are curious by nature; that the most efficient, long-lasting, and profound learning takes place when started and pursued by the learner; that all people are creative if they are allowed to develop their unique talents; that age-mixing among students promotes growth in all members of the group; and that freedom is essential to the development of personal responsibility. (Sudbury Valley School, n.d.).

Eventually, Peter and I both turned around. The more we read about it, the better we started to understand what this approach to schooling does for its students. We were determined to create a school on the same principles in The Netherlands. Today, there are three Sudbury schools in the country, and several other approaches to demo-cratic education are growing in other schools. Our children were, among others, the first to have benefited from this new type of education. In this chapter, I describe what democratic education is, and, more specifically, what a Sudbury school is all about and how it supports the development of a knowmadic worker.

Our daughter opened our eyes, showing us that the new generation needs to be treated differently, as our world is changing at an increasingly rapid pace. As discussed in the previous chapters, the world is moving away from a curriculum centered on fixed knowledge towards flexible knowledge, creativity, and co-creation based on different talents. That is why, in my opinion, education for Knowmad Society should support the development of skills needed to adapt quickly to the challenges and demands that a person certainly will face in the future world. We best do this by giving them the opportunity to learn to adapt, to deal with change, and to be prepared for anything. But, we do not prepare them for anything specific, which is a challenge to the current educational system.

Skills needed for a future enveloped in rapid change and ambiguity include: creativity, flexibility, and open-mindedness. This requires students that are naturally curious, not afraid to make mistakes, and intelligent in ways to quickly learn *new* knowledge and skills. Other traits include being a "self-starter," and showing initiative and entrepreneurialism, with the confidence to identify goals and make good decisions toward realizing them. This includes the development of self-esteem, self-confidence, and self-restraint to get to chosen goals. Finally, students need to be able to create new networks that are not dependent on physical borders or hierarchical structures (Hannam, 2012).

What approaches to education can best develop these students? In other words, how can we support a child best to adapt to perceived chaos and uncertainty of the unknown, and be successful? How can we best support a child in his or her development now for a world that will definitively have changed by the time he or she reaches maturity? How can we cope with our inability to know what knowledge is needed for future success in a world where uncertainty is the only certainty? Can we best do this through teaching? Or are there other ways, possibly better ways, in which we can support this development?

In a number of countries, projects have been initiated to identify skills needed for 21st century workers, and curricula have been designed to prepare children to learn these skills. In Cristóbal Cobo's earlier chapter on *Skills and competencies for knowmadic workers,* he extensively discussed a number of these projects. These are powerful examples that generally make a good synthesis of the situation. However, most of the projects make one fundamental error, they are focused on *adapting* the current educational system to meet current needs. They focus on redesigning schools, but not on reinventing the fundamentals of the educational paradigm. It is as if we are rearranging the deck chairs on the Titanic.

The basic assumptions for the need to change education are in line with what can be found elsewhere in this book. A fascinating quote is one made as an observation of the English and French national educational systems in the 19th century:

> National education [...] does not

seem at first sight to follow any kind of system, to be the logical product of an idea or preconceived plan; rather it seems to be the bizarre result of diverse and often contradictory forces; it appears to have developed from a purely coincidental accretion of traditions [...] and all of this is completely abandoned to individual initiative with the public authorities abstaining completely from any involvement. (de Bellaigue, 2004, p. 108)

The established school system is by no means evolved from any scientific basis; it just developed into what it has become today. But there is no reason to believe that this system is the only true system. In search for new educational approaches, we may have to move away from all that is so familiar to us. In order to move from a traditional system, we need new thinking, as the next quote suggests:

As a worldwide interdisciplinary project, the Classroom of the Future aims to bring together theorists and practitioners from various domains who join efforts to adapt the classroom to that which it can be expected to resemble in the 21st century. The pressure of change is on the classroom; it is utterly unthinkable that it can continue to be built, structured and equipped as it has been for all these decades. It is rather grotesque that societies, which essentially depend on and intently strive for innovation and progress, should try to source the power and energy for their innovative and progressive future from the physical and conceptual conditions of the educational mills of the 19th century. The Classroom of the Future aims to bridge this gap and to actively fashion this process of change with the help of educational scientists, media scientists, architects, designers, and teachers, to just name a few of those involved. (Mäkitalo-Siegl et al., 2009, p. 19)

Most of the educational renewal concepts are still designed around a standardized curriculum. The curriculum fixes "what" to learn and minimizes the scope for "how" to learn. The standard control systems are kept in place; compulsory tests and evaluations on "what" has been learned. In fact, focusing on testing takes away the opportunity to learn which is, in my opinion, the most important skill: being a creative problem-solver. Creativity is nurtured in situations of freedom, play, and joy; and, in situations where people face their own challenges by addressing real life problems without predefined outcomes.

John Holt (2012) states:

> No human right, except the right to life itself, is more fundamental than this. A person's freedom of learning is part of his freedom of thought, even more basic than his freedom of speech. If we take from someone his right to decide what he will be curious about, we destroy his freedom of thought. We say, in effect, you must think not about what interests you and concerns you, but about what interests and concerns us. (p. 179)

Holt (1974) believes a standardized curriculum for all creates a schooling industry that lacks individual thought and freedom of choice. He further argues such requirements and actions are in, "gross violation of civil liberties" (p. 25).

The greatest contradiction in school reform is that nobody is questioning the standardized curriculum. For this, we need people that are capable of envisioning new concepts of learning that connect with principles of natural human development, e.g., as stated in Ackoff and Greenberg (2008):

> Over the past 150 years, virtually everything has changed ... except education. Schools were designed as factories, to train factory workers. The factories are gone, but the schools have not changed. It's time for us to return to first principles ... or formulate new first principles ... and re-imagine education from the ground up. (back cover)

Ackoff and Greenberg, according to Gray (2008), go back to basic assumptions about education and our daily experiences, to consider how people learn, and how education might be restructured. The ideal schools Ackoff and Greenberg (2008) envision turn the modern idea of education on its head. According to them, "ideal schools represent a decentralization of education, and the devolution of the responsibility for each person's education to that person throughout life. These schools are built on the premise that each school is a self-governing community, with limitations imposed solely by the collective decisions of the community, and by the realities imposed by the outside world. But removing state, or other outside control over the educational functions of these schools does not remove the state's consti-tutional obligation to support each individual child's education" (p. 153). The question arises: *How did it come to be that schools in free democratic societies, like the United States, still condition children to be passive and to obey authority?*

In this light, it is striking that, in 1938, John Dewey already recognized the strength of participation by the learner:

There is, I think, no point in the philosophy of progressive edu-cation which is sounder than its emphasis upon the importance of the participation of the learn-er in the formation of the pur-poses which direct his activities in the learning process, just as there is no defect in traditional education greater than its failure to secure the active coopera-tion of the pupil in construction of the purposes involved in his studying. (Dewey, 1938, p. 72)

Hannam (2001) conducted a study on the effect of student participation in secondary schools. Twelve secondary schools in the UK were selected that were more than usually "student participative." These schools were traditional schools, in which attendance is compulsory and school cultures are often authoritarian. *The vocabulary of "uniform" and "discipline" at first sight seems to have more in common with a military environment than "a democratic society in miniature,"* according to Hannam (2001, p. 5). Moreover:

These schools, however, were on average doing better in "student participation" as for "learning to collaborate with others (peers and/or adults), in the identifica-tion of needs, tasks, problems within the school or the wider community, to ask appropriate questions and gather appropri-ate information, to discuss and negotiate possible courses of action, to share in planning and decision making, to share the responsibility for implementing the plan, to evaluate/review/reflect upon outcomes and to communicate these to others. (Hannam, 2001, p. 70)

He concludes that:

> The investigation confirmed the hypothesis that '...in schools that are already taking the 'participation and responsible action' elements of the Citizenship Order seriously for significant numbers of students of the full range of academic ability, an improvement in attainment would be found across the full range of GCSE results, though not necessarily mainly at the higher grades.' It further suggested that '... this might well be, in part at least, a consequence of higher self-esteem and a greater sense of ownership and empowerment of students leading to greater motivation to 'engage' with learning across the curriculum. (Hannam, 2001, p. 64).

If this positive effect is already acknowledged in traditional school settings, why isn't it applied to a wider range of schools? Why is it so difficult to accept the power of self-determination and self-realization? Is it because we think children are not capable of making wise decisions? And, is this a result from our own childhood experiences in which we were told that we were not able to make wise decisions

ourselves? Is that not, in itself, already a self-fulfilling prophecy? In moving to a new age, we desperately need to break with those perceptions and traditions.

According to Jef Staes (2010):

> The chaotic period in which we now live and work is the fascinating but dramatic transformation zone in which we are switching from the 2D to the 3D age. The flat two-dimensional (2D) age, characterized by classroom learning, predictability and continuous improvement, is laboriously making way for the three-dimensional (3D) age. The latter is an age in which increasingly passionate talent will result in groundswells of new information and innovation. (p. 58)

Staes further argues that we must tear down fences that make people behave as sheep, and promote a diploma-free educational system (Staes, 2011). He states there is demand for people that know their talents and know how to find information they need. Innovative organizations need a management style that can gather passionate people together around a common vision and allow them the freedom to use any source of information needed. They need to trust people. He believes we should give children and people personal responsibility in order to develop creative minds and creative behaviors.

Figure 4. "I expect you all to be independent, innovative, critical thinkers who will do exactly as I say!" (image by palomaironique)

THE PARADOX OF DESIGNING SCHOOLS FOR THE 21ST CENTURY >>

The paradox is, we are all products of a traditional schooling system, and we are tasked with trying to design a future-relevant education. This gravitates toward the reinforcement of old ideas, because our minds immediately translate the word "education" into the well-known environment in which we, ourselves, have been brought up. It is hard for us to imagine "education" occurring in different contexts.

Holt (1974) makes note of: "the right to learn, as opposed to being educated, i.e., made to learn what someone else thinks would be good for you" (p. 26). In principle, the word "schooling" has become synonymous with the word "education" in our minds. It is therefore very hard to imagine education as a place different from a situation where young people are divided into age groups, are told what to learn by a teacher, are tested for their knowledge with a pre-determined curriculum, and believe that "real" life starts after having passed the final exam. For the same reason, the word "teaching" has become synonymous with the word "learning," and the word "testing" has become commingled with "knowing." Therefore, it is hardly surprising that anybody is questioning the principle assumptions underlying our schools.

We need to invent a new language. Classrooms, age groups, teachers, lessons, timetables, curricula, tests, etc., all belong to the concept of "school" in our minds. This framework can hardly be left untouched as we seek to transform education. Usually, the reform is made by improving the curriculum incrementally (usually more of the same), increasing school hours, increasing requirements for exams, sometimes loosening the concept of classrooms by designing community learning centers, and by making use of new technology with the same purpose as we previously used books.

We need people that are capable of stepping out of this box, and who can look at the educational system from a distance. Or, in an expression attributed to Albert Einstein: "we can't solve problems by using the same kind of thinking we used when we created them." The paradox is that it is very hard to understand that we created a box, and that we are stuck in it. Our educational system has been so successful, that a vast majority of people all over the world has come to believe that this system is *the* only reality possible today.

Formal education was primarily designed to create an obedient workforce of factory workers and bureaucrats that could do the same job for hours at a time, day by day (Gatto, 2000). This compulsory educational system is based on the design developed by the totalitarian Prussian state in the 18th and early 19th century.

During the 18th century, the Kingdom of Prussia was among the first countries in the world to introduce tax-funded and generally compulsory primary education, comprising an eight-year course of primary education, called Volksschule. It provided not only the skills needed in an early industrialized world (reading, writing and arithmetic), but also a strict education in ethics, duty, discipline and obedience. Affluent children often went on to attend preparatory private schools for an additional four years, but the general population had virtually no access to secondary education. ("Prussian education system," n.d.)

Based on this model, the Prussian approach to education was emulated in a number of other countries, including those in modern democracies. An important aspect of the Prussian system was that it defined what children were to learn, what was to be thought about, how long to think about it, and when it is appropriate for children to think about something else. At its core, it was a system of thought control, and it established a presence in the psyche of the German elite that would later manifest into what we now refer to as mind control (Richman, 1994). This is, in my opinion, *brainwashing*.

From the beginning, public schools have been antagonists of liberty and the spontaneous order of a liberal market society. In such an order, individuals choose their own ends and engage in peaceful means, competitively and cooperatively, to achieve them. Parents also raise their children according to their own values and by utilizing their own judgment (Richman, 1994). In contrast, public schools are designed to interfere with this free development, and mold youth into loyal, compliant servants of the state. Their objectives have required a rigidity and authoritarianism that is inconsistent with the needs of nurturing a growing rational being that seeks knowledge about the world. Thus, schools are a source of immense frustration for many children. It should not surprise anybody that those schools produce children who are passive, bored, aimless, and even worse: self-destructive and violent. Schools today make use of new technologies and have adjusted their curricula around them, but the basics and purpose behind the schooling system are still to force children to learn and develop within certain pre-defined parameters (Gatto, 2002). Power resides within the government or the school, and not within the learner. Children are the slaves of this system; they still have to obey the orders of teachers, educators, and parents who were also products of this system. As Staes (2011) argues, our education systems are breeding lambs.

Another paradox is that teaching and testing of knowledge have become synonymous with the development of intelligence. In the past, building a vast amount of knowledge was highly valued. At that time, books were the only useful medium to store and retrieve information and every household with some status had an encyclopedia in the bookshelf. In those days, in many better-situated families, the boys were allowed to go to secondary school, high school, and university. Girls from those families, who were equally smart, often became teachers. A schoolmaster or teacher was someone with intelligence. Children could be motivated by the way a teacher could passionately talk about a subject, or talk about ideas that the teacher wanted to pass on. Over decades, standards for teacher training institutes lowered and increases in teachers' pay did not appear to have kept pace with those in other professions. Over the years, the job of the teacher devaluated, teaching standards have been introduced, and methods replaced the teacher's personal knowledge. Teaching itself became an industrialized process, based on methods and timetables, leaving barely any room for personal interpretations. School reform based on standardization and school accountability has a devastating effect in the classroom. It alienates children from the most important reasons to learn: their natural curiosity and motivation (McNeil, 2000).

Albert Einstein (in Hawking, 2009) reflected:

> One had to cram all this stuff into one's mind, whether one liked it or not. This coercion had such a deterring effect that, after I had passed the final examination, I found the consideration of any scientific problems distasteful to me for an entire year.... It is in fact nothing short of a miracle that the modern methods of instruction have not yet entirely strangled the holy curiosity of inquiry; for this delicate little plant, aside from stimulation, stands mainly in need of freedom; without this it goes to wrack and ruin without fail. It is a very grave mistake to think that the enjoyment of seeing and searching can be promoted by means of coercion and a sense of duty. To the contrary, I believe that it would be possible to rob even a healthy beast of prey of its voraciousness, if it were possible, with the aid of a whip, to force the beast to devour continuously, even when not hungry - especially if the food, handed out under such coercion, were to be selected accordingly. (p. 346)

This de-motivation effect can be devastating, and Einstein was not the only one who had suffered from it. There are many examples everywhere, where children are completely de-motivated from learning by schools. And, as Einstein is also attributed to have said: "It is a miracle that curiosity survives formal education." The need to do something about formal education to foster curiosity and motivation in learning is gaining increasing recognition. The question is, can we step out of our box, and design a new paradigm in education?

In order to transform our educational systems, we need to start looking with an open mind for evidence in different approaches already in practice. There are many examples of alternative educational designs, but one group that stands out and has grown over the past decades are *democratic schools*.

A DIFFERENT APPROACH TO EDUCATION: DEMOCRATIC SCHOOLS
>>

Democratic schools are designed around the concept that children are born into the world explicitly designed to educate themselves through their self-directed play and exploration. Much experience from all over the world has been gained from the schools that are specifically organized in such a way where children may take responsibility for their own learning and development (Gribble 1998). Democratic schools have existed since the early 20th century, and the Summerhill School in Suffolk, England, founded by A.S. Neill, is perhaps the oldest and best described in many books (see esp. Neill, 1995). In 1968, the Sudbury Valley School in Framingham, Massachusetts was founded. The designers of this school abandoned the idea of a fixed curriculum and modeled their school structure similar to the style of democracy practiced in New England town hall meetings (Greenberg et al., 1992). The Summerhill School is celebrated as being, "founded in 1921, still ahead of its time." That is probably correct for all democratic schools. In a world that is becoming increasingly dependent on creativity and the sharing of talents, schools should focus on on development of individual talents rather than collective knowledge.

Democratic schools recognize that kids are vibrant, energetic, interested, motivated, self-aware, and naturally inclined to learn (Gribble, 1998). Most of the students came from "traditional" schools and had to recover their natural self-esteem in their new learning environments. It sometimes takes weeks, months or even years to recover. And, luckily for them, their parents understand their need for a different approach. So, what makes democratic education so different? Moreover, what are the keys to its success?

PRINCIPLES OF DEMOCRATIC EDUCATION
>>

The basis of democratic education is centered on certain rights of students, which the European Democratic Education Community (EUDEC) defines as follows (based on the 2005 Resolution of the 13th International Democratic Education Conference); students have the right:

- To make their own choices regarding learning and all other areas of everyday life. In particular, they may individually determine what to do, when, where, how, and with whom, so long as their decisions do not infringe on the liberty of others to do the same.
- To have an equal share in the decision making as to how their organizations – in particular their schools – are run, and which rules and sanctions, if any, are necessary.

Specifically, EUDEC identifies regular democratic meetings with one-person, one-vote as a fundamental necessity of democratic education. Democratic schools are organized to allow students, from an early age on, to have an equal voice in the governance of their school. Most schools have weekly meetings, in which the school community makes decisions on governance issues. Because of this structure, students feel respected and empowered. The way the schools deal with rules, and more importantly, with breaking rules, is sometimes different. But, in general, a method is chosen in which the school deals with it democratically.

The basic need in free development is for a person to feel safe. Feeling safe in a community has a lot to do with a sense of justice, honesty, and being respected as a person. According to Maslow (1943), the basic safety needs are security, order, and stability. In traditional schools, safety is usually a policy, and actual safety is enforced top-down. Bullying is a common phenomenon in traditional schools, usually because of unequal relationships, peer pressure, unequal power, and a lack of a sense of responsibility (Strohmeier, 2008). In a typical democratic school, the sense of feeling safe is a responsibility of the entire community through a democratic process. People of all ages have the same responsibility to the community's rules and values.

Everyone is empowered, and respect for one another is valued highly. The sense of feeling responsible for your own community creates awareness. It is not said that the environment is completely peaceful, but the way the community deals with incidents that happen, often has a soothing effect. The democratic organization and process is the first important pillar on which these schools are built. This empowers a sense of responsibility over your own person and the community, the way you behave, the way you think, and the way you act. Physical and emotional safety is also protected by the absence of external stress enhancing factors, like test scores and curriculum. Figure 5 illustrates the essence of the most important parameters in relation to Ryan and Deci's (2000) self-determination theory (in Spaanbroek & Nijland, 2006).

Physical and emotional safety aids in the development of the second pillar: learning in a democratic school is self-determined. Students choose how to spend their school days, pursue their interests, and prepare themselves for their lives and careers. A democratic school is a learning community, where different age groups mix. In some schools, no age

Figure 5. Model for self-directed play and learning
(modified from Spaanbroek & Nijland, 2006)

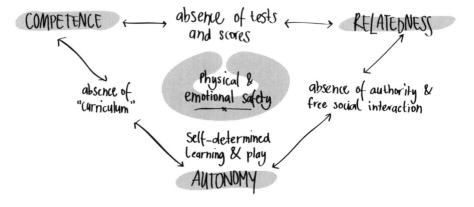

divisions exist. There are many ways to learn, including independent study, Internet-based research, playing games, volunteering, doing projects, visiting museums, traveling, and having discussions with friends and teachers. However, learning can also take place in classrooms, just like in conventional schools.

The way a school deals with intellectual freedom can vary between democratic schools. Some schools may require compulsory lessons; others make use of voluntary lessons or only provide lessons on request. The way schools give freedom of choice in learning is ultimately reflected in the level of responsibility at the general school meeting. In certain democratic schools, children share responsibility in the overall governance of the school, and, in other schools, they only have a say in their social world (Gribble, 1998).

In the matter of learning, motivation plays a vital role. Both internal (intrinsic) motivation and external (extrinsic) motivation types play distinguishable roles in learning. Intrinsic motivation is the natural, inherent drive to seek out challenges and new possibilities (Deci & Ryan, 2008). It is the most powerful driver behind learning.

In traditional schooling, extrinsic motivation is the most important driver for learning, in which the regulation of action has been partially internalized and is energized by factors such as a motive for approval, avoidance of shame, contingent self-esteem, and ego involvements. The goals established are not the goals of the "learner," they are the goals traditionally determined by the curriculum. In the traditional schooling approach, we have come to believe that we have to suffer in order to become educated.

Intrinsic motivation in learning emerges when an activity itself has value to a person (Deci & Ryan, 2008). I often hear people comment that a student in a democratic school will become lazy, that they will only do what is easy for them and only do things they feel passionate about. But in practice, students show a strong perseverance in doing hard stuff, not taking the easy way out. They know that they have to sometimes do, or learn, things that are not of their primary interest. But because they recognize the need for the knowledge or the skill, they accept the consequence of practicing hard. The difference is, that it is *their own choice*; they decide what is good for them at that moment.

Gribble (1998) concludes that what matters is that school graduates should be literate and numerate, of course, but also happy, considerate, honest, enthusiastic, tolerant, self-confident, well-informed, articulate, practical, co-operative, flexible, creative, individual, and determined people who know what their talents and interests are. They should have enjoyed developing their talents, and intend to make good use of them. They should be people who care for others because they have been cared for themselves. Students leaving democratic schools are more likely to fit this description, according to Gribble.

SUDBURY SCHOOLS

>>

Sudbury schools form a separate group of democratic schools and are modeled after the Sudbury Valley School. These schools practice a form of democratic education in which students are given complete responsibility over their education, which includes governance of the school. The entire school is designed in such a way that each student has personal responsibility and can act autonomously.

The school is run through a direct democratic process in a weekly school meeting in which students and staff members have an equal voice and an equal vote. In the school meeting, all decisions are made with great care, after vigorous and sometimes heated debates, by the vote of the majority. Everything that is voted on is real, including yearly staff elections. Most importantly, the boundaries to create a safe community are all set by the school meeting and violations of the rules are dealt with on a daily basis in each school's judicial committee.

Freedom in the school is experienced as a freedom of choice, a freedom of action, and a freedom to bear the results of action. Next to that, there is an unlimited intellectual freedom, to foster the development of individual talents and the value of individual choices. Students individually decide what to do with their time, and learn as a by-product of ordinary experience and much less from classes or lessons. There is a strong belief in the right of self-determination of students. Sudbury schools are therefore not working within a prescribed curriculum or schedule of classes, but work solely on the demands of students in their need to become acquainted with a certain subject. These subjects can be centered on anything, and need not necessarily have anything to do with a standard curriculum. Furthermore, Sudbury schools do not perform evaluations, assessments, or recommendations of any kind. Students can choose to make use of some tests for self-evaluation, but they are never used as external evaluation tools.

How do children learn in a Sudbury school? The concept of "intellectuality" has developed over time into a synonym for "book wisdom," steered by the knowledge bestowed by a curriculum. But, the principle behind some of the basic subjects in the curriculum has been related to the development of one's own mind. Challenging your own thoughts develops intellect, not book wisdom. In a Sudbury school, all people are treated with respect; there is no fear or barriers to interact with others. One is free to interact with whomever one wants, and discussions around various subjects take place constantly. This is where a great deal of wisdom is created, in addition to the traditional ways of discovering new information. Free interaction is everywhere, in the formal settings such as committee meetings, school-based corporations, or the school meeting. This also occurs less formally, whether it is sitting on a sofa, reading a book, playing a card game, taking a cooking class, or whatever activity the students choose.

For many people, the basic principles of a Sudbury school are often frightening. Trusting a kid, from the age of four years old, to educate him- or herself can be scary. If you visit a Sudbury school, you will see groups of children sitting and talking together, playing games, computing, running outside, playing a ball game, busy in the art or music room, and eventually you might find a few kids that take lessons, are reading or are gathered in some sort of "class." From the outside, it could appear to be a playground, and it could give the impression that nothing is really learned. But, in reality, a lot of learning takes place. In a Sudbury school, learning occurs most often in the "invisible" realm, as non-formal, informal, and serendipitous learning (Cobo & Moravec, 2011). Formal learning only takes place on certain occasions, but it is very limited. For this, age mixing and freedom to determine what to do are essential. As my eldest daughter explained to me, "you learn how to make use of knowledge at the moment you need it; there are no borders in learning anything, and you know that you can." This is, in essence, the skill that is developed – the underlying ability to cope with all circumstances.

HOW DO SUDBURY SCHOOLS PREPARE FOR KNOWMAD SOCIETY?
>>

TO BECOME LIFE-LONG LEARNERS

The Sudbury Valley School successfully opened in a period when the technology of today was not yet invented. The principles behind learning in such a school do not seem to be related to technology. Age mixing, in my opinion, is the most essential element in a Sudbury school. Most Sudbury learning takes place during formal and informal discussions and in communications between people of different ages and/or with different knowledge and experiences. This is crucial for building a worldview that is flexible and challengeable. It is also crucial in developing an open mind, critical thinking, and becoming an articulate communicator. Apart from that, learning takes place in almost anything you do, may it be reading a book, playing a video game, organizing an excursion, watching someone else do something, cooking, playing sports, or even daydreaming. These basic principles did not change over the decades. Modern technologies have also made a huge difference for Sudbury schools. Although the essential elements for learning did not change, the availability of technologies enable the creation of a greater spectrum for self-directed learning in the school. In fact, the Internet permits new possibilities for information exchange and provides new ways to develop knowledge and skills.

It has become increasingly obvious that learning is not something that occurs only in schools, but occurs anywhere and anytime. The community is no longer necessarily restricted to the school, itself,, but communications and discussions or other social interactions can continue anywhere and anytime. Because of the freedom provided in a Sudbury school, students can make full use of technological advances. They skill themselves in becoming a knowmadic worker, a person who knows how to develop the necessary skills needed, and who knows where to get information and how to co-operate with people in developing new ideas and expressing creativity. They have a great sense of self, have the courage to make choices, and seek training that is in line with their own needs.

Another aspect that makes a huge difference with respect to the added value of modern technology is the enormous impact that real-time, interactive computer games have on the development of social skills, intellectual- and strategic thinking, and language acquisition. Students today are well aware of the "world" around them. They learn foreign languages not because they are told to, but they learn them because it is essential for them. This is true for anything else they learn as well.

In The Netherlands, as in many other countries, learning at least one foreign language is essential. Kids are very aware of that. My own children learned to understand, speak and read English without one single formal lesson. As a parent and staff member, I was not aware that they did. But, by asking them later, they told me that they learned it by watching English-language television programs, playing games, and by reading Harry Potter and other books in English. Recently, a young boy showed extraordinary language skills in English as he simultaneously translated the entire 90 minute proceedings of the school judicial committee from Dutch to English

for a British visitor, which included a number of technical terms which many English children would have difficulty with understanding in their own language! He never took a formal lesson, and he is totally engaged with playing online computer games. Most of those games are in English, and a large understanding of the language is needed in order to take advantage of the experience. Another example is the story of a student in our school learning Japanese. She practiced by watching Japanese cartoon movies, first with subtitles, now without. On top of that, she started to learn Mandarin Chinese characters and Korean. Young students teach themselves how to read, just because they need it in the school to understand all the written matter or because they're interested in it and think it is fun to master. One of our youngest students is learning how to count, not only in Dutch, but also in the Frisian language and in English at the same time. She practices the entire day, asks other students for their age, and puts their age in line with her row of numbers. Nobody tells her to do that, and nobody provides encouragement to do so. But, everybody is willing to answer her questions and to give her the attention she asks for. Sometimes she makes mistakes, but she is her own evaluator.

We underestimate the innate processes of learning (Gray & Feldman, 2004), and likewise miscalculate the enormous drive children have to master their world and finally master anything that they need to survive in a constantly changing world. In a free environment without any compulsory guidance or pre-set goals, they learn to become life-long learners. Students, like adults, appear to be drawn together by common interests and play styles, personal attraction, and complementary desires to nurture and be nurtured (Gray & Feldman, 2004). Further analyses in Gray and Feldman's article identified apparent contributions of such interactions to both parties' physical, intellectual, and social/ moral education. Adolescents led children to act within the latter's "zones of proximal development" (term defined by Vygotsky, 1978) and children stimulated adolescents to make implicit knowledge explicit, be creative, and practice nurturance and leadership. These skills are invaluable for life-long learners.

TO BECOME CREATIVE MINDS

Free play is another important part of time spent in a Sudbury school. Free play is defined as an action that is chosen freely and has no pre-defined rules or outcomes. When children are together without interference of adults, they usually know how to play freely. Free play is essential in the development of 1) interests and competencies; 2) making decisions, solving problems, exerting self-control, and following rules; 3) learning to regulate emotions; and, 4) working together and experiencing joy (Gray, 2011). Play arouses curiosity, which leads to discovery and creativity.

Children who play do not draw an artificial line between work and play, according to Ackoff & Greenberg (2008). In principle, adults that are involved in work that they really enjoy experiencing the same emotions as we recognize in free play. Such a person is motivated, enthusiastic, attached, challenged to find solutions, and is creative in looking for solutions. Free play, according to Tim Brown, is an essential element in experiencing the freedom to be creative (TED, 2008).

Most of the workplaces are not designed to give people the freedom to experience play in work, and is probably one of the most important aspects for the lack in creativity and the resistance against change in organizations.

EXPERIENCE WITH DE KAMPANJE SUDBURY SCHOOL
>>

In the years since we started the De Kampanje Sudbury School in Amersfoort, we have experienced a lot of fun by being part of a wonderful community of people. Running a school may not be easy at times, and it forms a challenge, but it is very rewarding. We sometimes take in kids that are severely damaged by the regular school system. They lost their self-esteem, their motivation to learn, and, on top of it all, they have lost their trust in adults. They need to be left alone. We do not interfere with their daily activities. We make contact – we talk – but without any coercion or demands. After some time, you see them start to open up, interact with others, and dare to speak out their thoughts, wishes, and beliefs. For some of them, it takes years to recover from their negative experiences. It is a balance, and it needs an enormous amount of trust from parents as well. But, as soon as they know that they can trust the people in the school, they will feel safe enough to express their needs. They grow up being able to make their own choices. Some choose to take exams, some leave school to join vocational or high school, and some choose to work for a few years (including as entrepreneurs). But, for all of them, their motivation and self-knowledge steered them toward reaching their goals. Our operational record is still short, but the first signs of success are present.

As a staff member, it is always easier to trust a child, because we see that child every day, and we notice how he or she is doing. For parents, it is much harder. Parents often do not have the opportunity to see what their children are doing, and, most of the time, their children do not tell. From a parent's perspective, letting go is difficult. Not being able to ask at home what the child has been doing or to form an opinion on his or her activity is challenging. Even unspoken expectations a parent might have will form a dilemma for a child to feel really trusted and free. This adds to the pressure that a child feels from friends, grandparents, etc. The supportive role of the parents is crucial in the success of the child in a school like ours.

Last year, we hosted a boy in our school who stayed only for one year. He found himself some friends with whom he could play a certain online computer game, and played for a solid year. After this period, he decided to continue in regular school to prepare for his finishing exam. Back in the formal system, he interviewed successfully, and was able to express his motivations and wishes in a very articulate way. His parents were astonished; they saw such a tremendous change in his whole attitude in only one year. On the last day in our school, I told him that I hoped that he benefited from his experience with us. Then he said to me, "I was able to think over carefully what I really wanted this year." Just imagine, I only watched him playing computer games for this whole year. As outsiders, what do we really know is going on in the heads of these young people? Trust and freedom produce results that seem magical.

IN CONCLUSION
>>

There is a growing demand in society for alternatives to the regular educational system. Although The Netherlands is famous for its diverse schooling options (i.e., Montessori, Waldorf, Dalton, Freinet, Jenaplan, etc.), most of the options have become standardized by the governmental regulations for public schools over the past decades. As a result, these schools moved away from their initial pedagogical approaches. The government is placing more and more emphasis and pressure on testing and exams. The system, itself, is outdated, and more kids are suffering, both physically or by being labeled and over-cared for. As a result, student motivation is decreasing. The time is ripe to develop real alternatives to the mainstream model.

A new era has begun, and, more than ever, there is a demand for innovative, creative thinkers. Society needs people that can adapt to a fast-changing world in which we do not yet know what kind of skills will be needed to be successful in the future. The only way to educate our kids is by letting them experiment with uncertainty. Our education systems need to make a U-turn. Continuing the practices we have been engaged in the past few centuries is out of the question. In order to find a new educational model, we need to diversify, and resist uniformity (which has been the practice for the past decades in many countries).

Democratic education is an example of an approach that has changed the concepts of "schooling." These schools made the U-turn nearly a hundred years ago. They took education back to whom it once belonged: to the learner. By doing so, they made use of natural human abilities, by creating the circumstances for self-directed learning. They survived in the shadow of the traditional schooling system, which had created an efficient process to keep itself sustained. It is time that the world accepts democratic schooling as a valid, alternative approach for learning.

Democratic schools, and more specifically, Sudbury schools, are believed to support the development of skills that are essential in Knowmad Society. These schools are designed around freedom and responsibility. In

Sudbury schools, the responsibility is real. This fosters the development of skills that are essential to knowmadic workers. Children grow up as self-starters, showing initiative and entrepreneurialism, knowing how to use knowledge, their talents and how to make decisions on the basis of their own judgments. They know how to steer their lives with the guidance of their own inner compass, and make use of all resources needed to fulfill their goal. They have developed self-confidence, can work effectively together with people of all ages, and take responsibility for their choices and actions.

REFERENCES

Ackoff, R. L., & Greenberg, D. (2008). *Turning learning right side up: Putting education back on track*. New Jersey: Pearson Prentice Hall.

de Bellaigue, C. (2004). Behind the school walls: The school community in French and English boarding schools for girls, 1810–1867. *Paedagogica Historica, 40*, 107–121.

Cobo, C., & Moravec, J. W. (2011). *Aprendizaje invisible: Hacia una nueva ecología de la educación*. Barcelona: Laboratori de Mitjans Interactius / Publicacions i Edicions de la Universitat de Barcelona.

Deci, E. L., & Ryan, R. M. (2008). Self-determination theory: A macrotheory of human motivation, development, and health. *Canadian Psychology, 49*(3), 182–185.

Dewey, J. (1938). *Experience and education*. New York, NY: Kappa Delta Pi.

European Democratic Education Community - EUDEC (2005). Guidance document. Retrieved September 24, 2012 from www.eudec.org/Guidance+Document#Article_1:00_Preamble

Gatto, J. T. (2000). *The underground history of American education* (2nd ed. edition). New York: Odysseus Group.

Gatto, J. T. (2002). *Dumbing us down: The hidden curriculum of compulsory schooling*. Gabriola Island, Canada: New Society Publishers.

Gray, P. (2011). The decline of play and the rise of psychopathology in children and adults, *American Journal of Play, 3*(4), 443-463.

Gray, P., & Feldman, J. (2004). Playing in the Zone of Proximal Development: Qualities of self-directed age mixing between adolescents and young children at a democratic school. *American Journal of Education, 110*(2), 108-145.

Gray, S. D. (December 12, 2008). Taking learning seriously. [Review of the book 'Turning learning right side up', by R. L. Ackoff & D. Greenberg]. Retrieved September 24, 2012 from www.amazon.com/Turning-Learning-Right-Side-Education/product-reviews/0132887630/

Greenberg D., Greenberg H., Greenberg M., Ransom L., White A., & Sadofski, M. (1992). *The Sudbury Valley School experience*. Framingham, MA: Sudbury Valley School Press.

Gribble, D. (1998). *Real education, varieties of freedom*. Bristol, UK: Libertarian Education.

Hannam, D. H. (2001). *A pilot study to evaluate the impact of the student participation aspects of the citizenship order on standards of education in secondary schools*. London: CSV – retrieved from www.csv.org.uk/sites/default/files/Impact%20of%20Citizenship%20Education%20Report.pdf

Hannam, D. H. (2012). *Internal contra-inspection report for the use in the high court case of De Kampanje.* Unpublished manuscript.

Hawking, S. (2009). *A stubbornly persistent illusion: The essential scientific works of Albert Einstein.* Philadelphia, PA: Running Press.

Holt, J. (1974). Escape from childhood. In James Wm. Noll (Ed.), *Taking sides; clashing views on educational issues* (pp. 25-29). Dubuque, IA: McGraw-Hill.

Holt, J. (2012). The right to control one's learning. In S. J. Collins, H. Hazlitt, J. Hunt, S. Dodd, & W. McElroy (Eds.), *Everything voluntary: From politics to parenting* (pp. 179-184). USA: CreateSpace.

International Democratic Education Conference (IDEC). (2005). IDEC 2005 conference. Retrieved September 24, 2012 from: en.idec2005.org/

Jolles, J. (April 2012). Drie op de tien brugklassers: 'Ik kan of mag niet uitblinken op school'. Retrieved from www.learn.vu.nl/nl/nieuws-agenda/nieuwsarchief/2012/brugklassers-niet-uitblinken.asp

List of Democratic schools. (n.d.). In Wikipedia. retrieved September 24, 2012 from en.wikipedia.org/wiki/List_of_democratic_schools

Mäkitalo-Siegl, K., Zottmann, J., Kaplan, F., & Fischer, F. (2009). *Classroom of the future (technology enhanced learning).* Rotterdam, The Netherlands: Sense Publishers.

Maslow, A. H. (1943). A theory of human motivation. *Psychological Review, 50*(4), 370-396.

McNeil, L. M. (2000). *Contradictions of school reform.* New York: Routledge.

Neill, A. S. (1995). *Summerhill School: A new view of childhood.* New York: St. Martin's Griffin.

Pink, D. H. (2009). *Drive: The surprising truth about what motivates us.* New York: Riverhead Books.

Prussian education system. (n.d.). In Wikipedia. Retrieved September 24, 2012 from en.wikipedia.org/wiki/Prussian_education_system

Richman, S. (1994). *Separating school & state: How to liberate America's families.* Virginia: Future of Freedom Foundation.

Ryan, R. M. & Deci, E. L. (2000). Self-determination theory and the facilitation of intrinsic motivation, social development and well-being. *American Psychologist, 55*(1), 68-78.

Spaanbroek, L. & Nijland, L. (2006). *Alle dagen pauze: Analyse en beproeving van het theoretisch concept onder radicale onderwijsinnovaties.* Leiden, The Netherlands: Universal Press.

Staes, J. (2011). *Ik was een schaap.* Schiedam, The Netherlands: Uitgeverij Lannoo nv, Tielt en Scriptum.

Staes, J. (November 2010). Organisations in trouble: The 2D sheep drama. Retrieved from www.thefifthconference.com/files/TheFifthConference_PEOPLE_web.pdf

Strohmeier, D. (2008). Bullying and its underlying mechanisms. Retrieved from: www.education.com/reference/article/reasons-for-bullying/

Sudbury Valley School (n.d.). Sudbury Valley School: The cutting edge school for independent children. Retrieved September 24, 2012 from www.sudval.org

Summerhill school (n.d.). A.S Neill's Summerhill School. Retrieved September 24, 2012 from summerhillschool.co.uk/

TED (producer). (2008). Tim Brown: Creativity and play. Retrieved from www.ted.com/talks/tim_brown_on_creativity_and_play.html

Vygotsky, L. (1978). Interaction between learning and development. In M. Cole, V. John-Steiner, S. Scribner, & E. Souberman (Eds.), *Mind in society: The development of higher psychological processes* (pp. 79-91). Cambridge, MA: Harvard University Press.

Notes

Notes

Notes

DRAW
your
IDEA
HERE

Notes

Notes

Knowmads Business School: Empowering and enabling knowmads

PIETER SPINDER

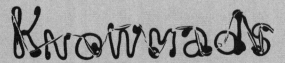

Figure 6. Knowmads Business School logo

'EVERYBODY HAS A FIRE FOR SOMETHING. WE BREATHE IN FRESH OXYGEN TO START THE FIRES OF OUR STUDENTS, AND UNBELIEVABLE STUFF HAPPENS.'

Whoosh!

DIRECTOR & OWNER

'KNOWMADS IS NOT A DRESS REHEARSAL. WE CREATE REAL STUFF.'

PIETER SPINDER

'WORK TO MAKE THINGS HAPPEN.'

'Knowmads Business School takes you on a journey, and together we get inspired to make a difference and a change in our lives and in the lives of others.'

SUMMARY

KNOWMADS BUSINESS SCHOOL:
EMPOWERING AND ENABLING KNOWMADS
- Pieter Spinder -

The idea of the *Knowmads Business School* in Amsterdam began in June 2009, with four people who were previously involved in the Kaospilot Netherlands post-graduate program and the University of Applied Sciences of Amsterdam. Originating from our experiences through our work in the field of education, we wanted to do something meaningful and different, based, among other insights and desires, on the idea that we need to help young people develop skills and attitudes that are relevant for the modern world.

To us, it seemed strange to have a program with a fixed curriculum that lasted a traditional period of three to four years, while the transformations taking place in the rest of the world were happening much faster. When creating Knowmads, we did not want to approach students as empty buckets to be filled with knowledge. We instead consider them as young professionals. We wanted to give them the possibility to co-create with partnering companies and institutions, and make use of the knowledge that already exists. We had many questions, and we had no answers. Our program is implemented by Knowmads staff and by our invited lecturers/contributors. It is centered on co-creation among students, lecturers, and staff around various assignments. We connect this to people, and then design *with*, not *for*, to build and implement services and products that make the world a better place. By working with leaders in companies, big and small, we have the possibility to create together the changes that we think are needed. As stated before, Knowmads is not a dress rehearsal. We work on real assignments with the goal to create real value (e.g., money, knowledge, and sponsorships). We don't talk about case studies. *We create real stuff.*

The world is facing huge challenges, and they are growing daily, in severity, scale and in complexity. It is no exaggeration to say that they are not going to go away. Indeed, they will get worse, unless we start to find solutions, and we find them soon. If we are going to survive, we desperately need the next generation to be smarter, more adaptable, and better prepared than any that has gone before. Our only chance is to improve the way we teach our young; to equip our young people with the skills and the attitudes that might steer this world of ours to a far safer place than it presently looks likely. The question is, is that what our current education system does? (Introduction from Goodrich, 2009)

The beginning of the Knowmads Business School in Amsterdam

The idea of the *Knowmads Business School* began in June 2009, with four people who were previously involved in the Kaospilot Netherlands post-graduate program and the University of Applied Sciences of Amsterdam. Originating from our experiences through our work in the field of education, we wanted to do something meaningful and different, based, among other insights and desires, on the ideas that coincided with those presented by Daryl Goodrich (2009).

From our perspective, the current education system does not provide enough young people who can create change. Ecological, social, and economic transformations are taking place, and with "old," industrial approaches still lingering in business and education, we will not be able to transform to the extent we need to by looking at the situation as a "crisis" (Knowmads looks at it as *transformation*, much like nature manages to transform continuously). Transformation starts with personal transformation. When one has a connection with him- or herself, then one can make a connection with the outside world and with the surrounding environment.

To us, it seemed strange to have a program with a fixed curriculum that lasted a traditional period of three to four years, while the transformations taking place in the rest of the world were happening much faster.

And, what about personal learning needs? How is it possible to say that only in the third semester of the third year you are permitted to take a course in marketing, while it might be that a student already has a pressing need for it, is interested in it, or wants to take it during an earlier semester? Moreover, why work with case studies published in books, when one can learn from real challenges, real life assignments with companies, interactions with governments, and work with non-governmental organizations? Why make education a dress rehearsal, instead of an encounter with real life?

When creating Knowmads, we did not want to approach students as empty buckets to be filled with knowledge. We instead consider them as young professionals. We wanted to give them the possibility to co-create with partnering companies and institutions, and make use of the knowledge that already exists. We had many questions, and no answers.

That is when we decided to leap into action.

We wanted to do something different. We wanted to change the game of education, and bring something meaningful and beautiful into the world. Our aim was to bring joy into the field by guiding young people to follow their own passions, and work to make things happen which would bring smiles on their faces, ourselves, our collaborators, and our environment.

We constructed a framework based on our responses to four driving questions:

- In what world do we want to live? *Sustainability and social innovation.*
- What do I want to contribute/change? *Personal leadership.*
- How can I best organize to get it done? *Entrepreneurship and new business design.*
- How do I bring it in the world? *Marketing and creativity.*

We checked with John Moravec, father of the *knowmads* concept and terminology, if the idea of a school, as a platform, partly based on his theory about knowmadic living, learning, and working looked good to him. He was very happy about the idea, so we registered some domain names, built a website at **www.knowmads.nl**, and started to talk with potential business partners about our idea. We did not have a building; we did not have a program; we did not have students; we did not know who would facilitate it; and, we did not have money to launch the program. Fortunately, we recruited partners who liked the opportunity of getting to work together with a diverse group of young, international professionals on particular business challenges they were experiencing that related to the above four questions.

Recruited through our website, Facebook, Twitter, and informational meetings, 12 young people joined Knowmads in Amsterdam in February 2010. At our first application workshop, participants from the USA, Canada, Brazil, South Korea, Switzerland, Germany, and The Netherlands attended. This group had to tell their friends and parents they were going to attend a "school" in Amsterdam (we prefer to call it a "platform"). They did not know where it would be located within the city, had to pay a €4,500 entrance fee, and they had to acknowledge that Knowmads Business School was outside of the Dutch formal education system, so they could not receive an official diploma at the end of the program. We called this group the "Knowmads Pioneers." They wanted to challenge themselves and the outside world. They were the people who wanted to change the game. And, they did... and continue to do so in their professional work.

How we do things at the Knowmads Business School

Our program is implemented by Knowmads staff and by our invited lecturers/contributors. It is centered on co-creation among students, lecturers, and staff around various assignments. Our lecturers are always experts in their field, and throughout the year, students work on assignments for our partnering organizations. Our program has a few core workshops and tools that we offer to every team of students, such as: deep democracy, nonviolent communication, business model canvas creation, Startup Wheel, Chaordic Stepping Stones, sales, marketing, and project management. Other workshops support assignments or group processes knowmads students may be engaged in at any particular moment. In the first year, the students decided to form a legal entity together: Knowmads U.A. (a cooperative), which to this day is used by students as a vehicle to earn money through their completion of their real world assignments.

The Knowmads staff brings in four assignments per year, which connect explicitly to the four organizing questions. The students work on these together with leaders from each collaborating organization and/or one or more of their employees. After the partnering company delivers their challenge, the students create a working plan, which includes a financial proposal for services. Once the partner accepts the quote, the tribe (as the students started calling themselves) starts working, coached by the Knowmads staff. The aim is to create a win-win-win situation, for the students, for our partnering organization, and for our broader society. In addition to the program, we encourage our students to work on their own projects and businesses as practicing knowmads. One or more experts sourced from the Knowmads network also coach each student during the year.

The core points of our program is that we work, in our educational experiences and with the real life assignments, with our heads (knowledge), our hearts (feeling) and our hands (doing/action). We further work to connect these to idealism (dreams), talents, and other disciplines.

At Knowmads, we base our program year on individual learning needs, in a team-based environment, which is structured on modern organizational theories (see, e.g., Sharmer, 2007). During the first half-year, students experience a considerable amount of un-learning (a need to get rid of old patterns), and during this unlearning, we try to find the individual- and team-level knowledge needed to bring ourselves a step, or several steps, further in our learning journeys, so we can implement this in our daily practice.

The Internet is a basic working environment for Knowmads. We collaborate through online project management tools (e.g., DropBox), and maintain our own online video channels. Social media, such as Facebook and Twitter, are tools we cannot ignore if we wish to work

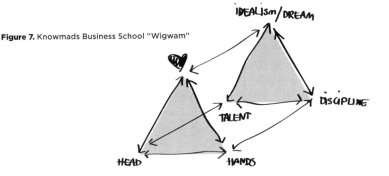

Figure 7. Knowmads Business School "Wigwam"

together. As the world becomes smaller and smaller through the application of technologies, and more accessible through online tools, we try to choose which collaborative technologies are the most useful to co-create with our partners and the community we serve.

We believe in bringing nice, good and inspiring things into the world, and inspiring through fun processes and projects that are beautiful and beneficial to the people and the planet we live on. We do these things at Knowmads because we believe in the power of "you reap what you sow." And, by doing so, we find that people return to us to do more good projects most of the time.

We can have an impact by being honest to ourselves, and by being honest to the outside world. We do not do things because we have been doing these practices for centuries, but we check within ourselves to determine what it is that we really want to do. We connect this to people, and then design with, not for, to build and implement services and products that make the world a better place. By working with leaders in companies, big and small, we have the possibility to create, together, the changes that we think are needed. As stated before, Knowmads is not a dress rehearsal. We work on real assign-ments with the goal to create *real value* (i.e., money, knowledge, and sponsorships). We don't talk about case studies. *We create real stuff.*

As every startup entrepreneur is aware, it is hard to start something completely from scratch. Especially since we are comprised as an original combination of educational and business approaches, we are no exception. Because the Knowmads Business School is a completely new concept, it is difficult for us to secure funding from traditional sources. We started two years ago with 12 students. In February 2013, we are planning to admit 15 new students, and, by then, 42 will have "graduated." Other institutions and startups around the world are already adopting the Knowmads concept. We are engaged directly with startups in Israel, and we are connected to the University of Applied Sciences in Amsterdam through a Knowmadic Learning Lab minor program.

Today, students pay an entrance fee of €5,500. With this money, we provide school grounds (a building to work in), Internet, coaching, process facilitation, and compensation for the people who come from inside and outside of the school to lead the assignment workshops. By working on our assignments, the students also have the potential to earn while they learn. We enroll new tribes of Knowmads twice a year, in August and February. By doing, so the tribes are very much connected, and there is a sense of community. One of the core beliefs of Knowmads is that there is a lot of invisible, peer-to-peer learning that occurs between tribes. Therefore, each half year, the more "senior" tribe has an opportunity to work on assignments and projects together from the newest tribe that joined the school.

After the one-year program, the students can choose to stay at the school to incubate their dream business (some of them do this already during the year), coached by Knowmads staff, in what we call the *Knowmads Greenhouse*. In the first year alone, our students, who worked on 50 assignments, started five companies. The staff brought only four of these assignments in.

Despite our "earning while learning" philosophy, it is hard to earn back the entrance fee, but this is seen by most of the students as a bonus – and a challenge. When we started Knowmads, it was important for us to set a balance in learning and earning. If we only did projects, we would become a "doing a project" school, which would not be ideal. Our approach is to get the students connected with the Knowmads community, which encourages them to find out where their passions are, why they want to bring something into the world, and how to do that by practicing and learning with real life assignments, and with real life companies.

What we did and do at Knowmads

The first two years ran by us rapidly, and we accomplished a lot. We offered over 125 workshops, including Seth Godin on "shipping," Moraan Gilad on deep democracy, Patrick van der Pijl on business model canvassing, Godert van Hardenbroek on sustainability in action, Kristian Harder on social media, Tsi-la Piran on personal leadership and spirituality in action, Charley Davis on money, Fokke Wijnstra on value-based working, Wim Vrolijk on sales, and more. Most of the workshops were conducted in an action learning format, to build an authentic connection with the themes of the assignment, and to apply the content of the workshop to the assignments we where working on. In an appendix to this book, you will find a list of key workshops we offered up to November 2012.

Here are Some of our early assignments for partnering organizations:

- We engaged in a creativity and marketing assignment for KLM Airlines, and pitched the concept of "social seating" (being able to review the LinkedIn and Facebook profiles of people seated near you on a flight so you may have a better chance of engaging in conversation with somebody you like).
- For Royal Haskoning, we worked on an assignment for making workplace sustainability visible in large corporate environments.
- For the WereldWinkels chain of fair trade shops in The Netherlands, we worked to reinvent fair trade marketing, and make it accessible and interesting for the broader public.
- We worked on an assignment for T-Mobile, and organized a Diversity Journey for 15 European human resource managers in Amsterdam.
- We developed content for the PICNIC Festival in Amsterdam.
- Achmea asked us to help them devise a launch for a special insurance product marketed toward self-employed workers.

...and, some 40 other bigger and smaller assignments – all in the first year.

The future of Knowmads

We believe that the solutions to some of the challenges humanity faces may be solved through creative and entrepreneurial behavior, and also on a platform where you work as you learn. By doing so, we work and learn with real assignments, and share our knowledge, feelings, and action within a diverse group of people. We love the way we do things, and we learn a lot by making mistakes. Knowmads is a learning organization, and shapes itself during the process when the process needs it. Just like real life.

We learn a lot during our lives. It is a long road with no end in sight, and there are mountains of invisible learning to be crossed. When one can catch his or her passion, find a way to get the knowledge and the skills to work with other people, young and old, we have a superb starting point.

Everybody has within him- or herself a fire for something. Some fires are big, some are smaller, and some just do not look like fire, but look like black coal. What we try to do at Knowmads is blow some air onto this coal, which everybody has inside of them. We breathe in fresh oxygen to start the fires within our students, and unbelievable stuff happens. Whoosh!

Knowmads, welcome home!

REFERENCES

Goodrich, D. (Director). (2009). We are the people we have been waiting for. UK: New Moon Television.

Scharmer, C. O. (2007). *Theory U: Leading from the emerging future* (1st ed.). Cambridge, MA: Society for Organizational Learning.

KNOWMADS STUDENTS AND STAFF WITH SETH GODIN, 2010

NOTES

Notes

notes

Getting from top-down to all-on-top

EDWIN DE BREE AND BIANCA STOKMAN

'THE OPERATING SYSTEMS OF HIERARCHICAL ORGANIZATIONS PREACH MEDIOCRITY, OBEDIENCE, AND DOCILITY.'

'The enablers of the 20th century are the disablers of the 21st century.'

'ADAPTABILITY IS A MATTER OF SURVIVAL.'

EDWIN DE BREE & BIANCA STOKMAN

'TO ACCELERATE PROGRESS, WE NEED TO LET GO OF OLD HIERARCHICAL MODELS.'

'ORGANIZING IS ALWAYS ABOUT CULTIVATING BEHAVIOR. STRUCTURE IS THE STAGE ON WHICH TALENT AND PASSION EXCELS OR NOT.'

SUMMARY

GETTING FROM TOP-DOWN TO ALL-ON-TOP
- Edwin de Bree & Bianca Stokman -

Birds gathering in flocks, fish swimming in schools, and wolves hunting in packs seem to follow a few simple, instinctive rules to create coherence in their groups. What rules do humans in organizations follow?

As we move toward a knowmadic society, new rules seem to apply. These differ from traditional, organizational structures, and these rules are perhaps more aligned with the "natural order" of human interaction. After all, we have developed many kinds of instinctive behaviors in dealing with other people in the course of our evolution. If we leave it to the (nature of) people instead of institutions, how would they organize themselves? And, is this self-organization effective?

We believe the emerging Knowmad Society has an immense impact on work and the way work is organized. In this chapter, we explore the following questions:

1   Can rules be formulated for the self-organization of people? What basic principles would we have to obey to come to an efficient and successful cooperation?

2   Can we design the context or structure of an organization in a way that every individual is encouraged to take on leadership and followership responsibilities, depending on which is best for the situation and task at hand?

3   How do the factors of social interaction in which the brain responds with feelings of stress or reward influence the way we organize ourselves in Knowmad Society?

Although traditional hierarchies and processes – which together form a company's 'operating system' – are optimized for day-to-day business, they can't handle the challenges of mounting complexity and rapid change. (Kotter, 2012)

Why we need to let go of hierarchies to create real acceleration

Businesses need to accelerate to keep up with the rapidly emerging changes in society. In this chapter, we explore what this means for workers and the companies in which they work.

We start with an exploration of the present needs of employees and the changing nature of their work within the context of the emergence of knowmadic workers. We then discuss a few examples of enterprises that are organized according to knowmadic principles, and look at what we can learn from them.

The knowmadic worker

The "knowmadic worker" is knowledgeable, is willing to share their knowledge, and is able to work together with a variety of people at varying locations. Technological progress enables him (or her) to work at any time, anywhere, and transform this knowledge into something you can use at anytime and anywhere. The number of knowmadic workers is increasing steadily, and this puts different demands on organizations. Knowmadic workers look for personal and professional development, autonomy and responsibility, optimal technological facilitation, and flexibility in work hours, to name a few. Traditional, hierarchical organizations do not seem to match these demands.

More and more people prefer a different kind of labor relationship to the traditional contract, including freelance employment, sometimes organized in a network structure, and small companies with a clear identity. It seems to be the result of an ever-growing need for self-actualization, autonomy, and emotional fulfillment. Big companies with a clear identity, who create a community of followers, are successful as well (i.e., Apple, Ikea, and Google). They tell an appealing story that people can relate to. It makes us want to be part of "the team," an important need for the human species.

The idea is not new. In the early 1980s, Peters and Waterman (1982) published an analysis of successful organizations. Companies that spend a lot of time, energy, and money on the "soft" aspects of business proved to deliver the best "hard" results. The authors categorized eight aspects of success that today are still very relevant: an excellent enterprise is biased for action, close to the customer, stimulates autonomy and entrepreneurship, values its people,

is value-driven, stays with the core business, and keeps its staff lean, and combines centralized values with decentralized autonomy. The question is, if their book, *In search of excellence*, was written thirty years ago; how is it possible that not every enterprise has followed its conclusions? Apparently, the sense of urgency to adapt these views is low. Our presumption is that in Knowmad Society this sense of urgency will grow. The tension between the needs and wants of the laborer and the conditions that traditional organizations offer will increase.

This chapter first takes a look at the evolution, biology, and neurology of human interaction, and the implications for leading and following. What are the patterns in our social exchanges? We place these patterns in the perspective of Knowmad Society. Is the knowmadic paradigm of working and learning aligned with our biology? What does it mean for existing hierarchical organizations and institutions? How can they make the transition toward becoming *knowmadic organizations*?

Nature rules

Search for "spreeuwen Utrecht" on YouTube.com, and you'll find a beautiful video of a flock of starlings over Utrecht,

The Netherlands. The flock moves as one dancing cloud, seemingly connected through an invisible magnetic field. A peregrine attacks, and the flock apparently decides as one mind to split up and move out of the way, after which the separate clouds melt into unison as soon as the peregrine is gone. What moves them? Which laws are they obeying? How can they fly so close and not fly into each other? The same questions apply to a school of fish or a pack of wolves on the hunt. These processes and questions are amply researched. For example, a pack of wolves hunts following two principles:

- Get as close to the prey as is possible without risking bodily harm; and,
- Stay as far away from the other wolves as possible

This way, the prey can be exhausted without escaping, and the wolves are not in any danger. Whether birds, insects, or fish, these kinds of rules are researched or discovered for each of these species. Craig Reynolds (2001) developed a program in the 1980s that simulated the movement of fish and birds in a school or flock. He called the moving triangles in his simulation "boids," and came up with three rules they have to obey in order to function in what he called the swarm:

1 Keep enough distance as not to get in another's way, and change direction to avoid collision;
2 Move in the same direction as your nearby swarm members; and,
3 Make sure there is cohesion, and stay near to your nearest swarm mates.

This is sometimes called *swarm intelligence* (SI) and is based on the collective behaviors of decentralized, self-organizing systems, natural or artificial. This rules-based system is used for computer games, solving traffic dilemmas, and in the production of animation films. Another way of looking at SI is provided by Krause et al (2009, p. 29). They state that SI is, "a mechanism that individuals use to overcome some of their own cognitive limitations," and that, "not all collective behavior should be regarded as evidence of SI."

These principles of biology have enjoyed a renewed interest in the past decade within the management and organizational development literature, which concern our social organization patterns. Social neuroscience is a relatively new field that combines biology, psychology, and neurology to gain more knowledge on how we, as humans, interact. Evolution contributes to this knowledge by addressing the function of specific behaviors. The basic idea is that only those behaviors are passed on genetically which play a role in the survival of the species.

Can rules be formulated for the self-organization of people? What basic principles would we have to obey to come to an efficient and successful cooperation? You can get a glimpse of this on YouTube as well. Look for almost any video on crossing the road in urban India; the video will resemble that of the birds and fish. No traffic lights, no pedestrian crossings, no apparent rules: a multitude of people finds their way to the other side of the road, and usually without incident. However, we are intelligent creatures, aren't we? We have the capability to reflect on our own behavior. Undoubtedly, humans don't follow a few simple biological rules when it comes to their interaction, right?

Evolution

It's not news to anybody that humans are animals. We eat, mate, defecate, sleep, breathe, and procreate. We like to compare ourselves to animals: we are as sick as a dog, as hungry as a horse, or as gentle as a lamb. We have butterflies in our stomach, and a memory like an elephant. It gets more interesting when we look at our social interactions from a biological viewpoint as well. We like to think of ourselves as a higher order creature, and not as a simple animal.

After all, because of our prefrontal cortex (the part of our frontal lobe that is responsible for much of our rational processes) we are capable of metacognition, and reflection on the interaction between our "me" and "our surroundings." Because of that, we should be able to control ourselves and put things into perspective, wouldn't you say?

What does separate us from the other animals? Frankly, science hasn't come up with a clear answer to the question. Going from monocellular to multicellular structures, there probably were some accidental cell divisions that lead to more complex brain structures. About 200 million years ago, these developed into the first mammals, already equipped with a small cerebral cortex. This enabled them to perform more complex movements. They were mainly nocturnal. The brain areas for touch and smell developed first, according to fossil findings. Following the extinction of dinosaurs approximately 65 million years ago, some mammals expanded their territory to the trees. They were the ancestors of primates. Relying more on their sight while moving through the trees, the visual cortex became more important. In addition, since they lived in strong social structures, the volume of the frontal cortex increased as well. Social interaction is intensive in energy consumption, and the brain needed complex structures to do it well.

The brain is an efficient organ. However, the more impulses it receives, the more it starts looking for underlying patterns to speed up information processing. This might explain the presence of our subconscious and our incredibly fast ability to analyze and react. From this point on, the development of the brain was probably an interrelated string of events, leading from more-refined motor functioning to provide better food, to continued brain growth, to better living conditions, and so on. Finally, 200,000 years ago, the first humans began walking on African soil (Robson, 2011).

In short, during the time that we walked around on two legs, our neurological structures have formed and adjusted to help our biological system (body) survive as best it could. This applies not only to our interactions with the surrounding flora and fauna, but also to our interactions with other people. Our knowledge on social interactions, on the feelings of another person, and on safety and threat has become part of our hardware. What we see, hear, smell, taste or feel is crucial in our functioning. It is fascinating to think how all these structures in our bodies have developed in a trial and error fashion, stemming from interaction with, and adjustment to, our surroundings – survival of the fittest.

Followership and leadership

People have always lived in communities. From an evolutionary point of view,

that is the wisest choice. We are not the largest, not the strongest, and not the fastest species alive. It takes a long time before our offspring can take care of themselves. Together, we are much stronger. In case of sickness or physical threat, the members of our groups can protect and take care of each other. Being part of a group, we stand a much better chance to survive and therefore pass on our genes to the next generation.

The small, nomadic groups that long ago lived on the savanna knew that a system of leaders and followers helped them deal with social issues like the collection and preparation of food and creating a place to spend the night (see van Vugt & Ahuja, 2011). The benefit for the leader was that it led to increased status, more rewards like access to the best food and bed, and more sex. For the follower, it meant the benefit of protection by the leader and the group. This was a mutual agreement that leads to satisfactory results for both.

Leadership and followership appear to have developed into the "natural order of things," and have become part of our hardware in the millennia that followed. The group member who was good at following had a better survival rate and passed on the "follower genes." The genes of the group leader who was followed best were also best passed on. These processes created genetic programs for "follower" and for "leader" (van Vugt & Ahuja, 2011). Leadership exists, according to van Vugt and Ahuja (2011), as a result of followership. The leader is the one who is best suited for the specific task at hand (i.e. the best hunter or the strongest warrior), and is followed because of that. Leadership is not necessarily limited to one person, but can be divided over different people, depending on the division of tasks. The followers determine the leadership. There is a great example of this on YouTube as well, search for a video called, "Leadership from a dancing guy."

So, followership pays off, and creates a better survival rate for the follower genes. Solitary behavior has a harder time surviving. Not only is the loner at a greater risk to run into personal danger, he also cannot learn about more effective behavior to deal with his surroundings by looking at the actions of other group members. Followership is therefore widespread. There are more followers than leaders; and, in times of uncertainty and crisis, there is a cry for leadership and direction in business as well as in other areas of society.

Followership-enabled leadership could be interpreted as traditional organizational structures being the best suited for our biology. It connects with a human need to be lead, and every echelon gets its leader. It's true that this traditional structure offers a context that appeals to the biological need for leadership and followership. However, this structure turns a fluid need into a solid solution; leadership for a vast range of tasks is attributed to one person instead of being divided among the most suited people per task. An organization that is truly aligned according to "bio-logic" does not deny the need for leadership and followership, but stimulates the distribution of leadership in line with the capacities of people.

In the framework of Knowmad Society, and with the idea that behavior develops in adjustment to surroundings, this leads to the following question: *can we design the context or structure of an organization in a way that encourages every individual to take on leadership and followership, depending on which is best for the situation and task at hand?*

Social neuroscience

With evolution and group behavior in mind, it doesn't make sense to study a human being by itself. Our brain develops in constant interaction with its (social) surroundings. If we really want to understand how the brain works, then it has to be researched not as a solitary phenomenon, but as a social organ, part of and coherent with other brains. In the same way, our individual body is a coherent system of billions of cells which we do not normally research from the perspective of a single cell. This idea is the basis of social neuroscience.

As stated earlier, we aim to be as effective as possible in handling our context so that we have a better chance at survival. We constantly scan our surroundings for that purpose. Every second, thousands of impulses enter through our senses. We register, process, and interpret these impulses, and, if necessary, turn them into action. Many of these impulses come from people around us. Emotions are an important factor in this interpersonal exchange. Fear we read on another person's face can point out the danger somewhere near us. Repulsion can warn us not to eat a specific food. In a social setting, emotions and facial expressions also communicate information on our social status (Schutter & den Boer, 2008). We especially judge all impulses on their level of possible threat or possible reward. In many cases, we are not even aware that this judgment takes place, but our physiological signals give us away (Williams et al., 2006). The higher the level of threat or reward, the higher is the need for action. Both have

to do with survival. We need to act when we fear harm, but we also need to act when we have a chance, for instance, to obtain great, nourishing food, social satisfaction, or sex.

To motivate us to act, our brain mainly uses two important systems. The brain reward system (BRS) motivates us to move towards a stimulus and to action. The most important neurotransmitter in the BRS is dopamine. When we are doing something that is good for our survival, like eating or having sex, dopamine is released. It gives us a sensation of pleasure, it helps us focus our attention, and it motivates us to repeat this behavior (Nuytten, 2011). However, we tend to get used to dopamine, so the BRS needs more and more stimulation to achieve the same level of pleasure.

When we experience a potential threat to our existence, the amygdala (an almond shaped organ in the middle of our brain) starts up a stress response that includes the release of cortisol. This neurotransmitter prepares our body for action and motivates us to create distance between the threat and ourselves. First, it sharpens our judgment of the threat, second it prepares us to handle the threat if necessary: fight or flight. Third, cortisol helps us to remember the situation. That way, we can prevent it from happening again, by noticing it sooner or avoiding it altogether. This does not happen when the threat is too overwhelming, however. The experiences that we memorize eventually lead to wisdom and intuition (Ratey, 2008).

It's not only the physical stimuli like sex, food, spiders, or snakes that lead to a release of dopamine or cortisol. There are aspects of social interaction that result in the same neural experience of pleasure or pain. Through these systems of reward or distress, our brain can encourage us to move toward or away from another person or a situation, or to engage in different kinds of behavior.

Social interaction

The model we will use to describe pain and reward in social interaction is the SCARF-model by David Rock (2008), founder of the NeuroLeadership Institute. In the SCARF model, Rock categorized five factors of social interaction to which the brain reacts in a similar way as to primary physical threats or possible reward:

- **S**tatus
- **C**ertainty
- **A**utonomy
- **R**elatedness
- **F**airness

Status

Status concerns the relative position of an individual in a group. It is the way the individual perceives the position that matters. The question, "am I higher or lower in status than the others?" is important. The more positive the perception of our rank is, the more pleasurable the situation. From an evolutionary point of view, when we are making a positive contribution to the group, we can be more at ease about our survival because we are part of that group. A negative ranking, however, is threatening, and leads to stress. It is the weakest link that is most attacked in a herd. So, it's not so much about hierarchy, but about perception of our status. We estimate our added value in groups by assessing our knowledge and experience, our ideas and input, and our feeling of being a "better" person than someone else. It is easy to feel threatened by our status, and it is easy to threaten someone else, even if we do not want to. We can do it by sounding intimidating, when we explain something that did not need an explanation, or when we tell someone how to do his or her job. We can even threaten status just by asking, "may I give you some feedback?"

The good news is we can also enhance a person's perception of status quite easily by acknowledging their improvement at a task and sharing compliments, preferably when others are present. An organization where it is clear for every individual what his or her added value is, where focus is on strength, and where possible weaknesses are discussed openly and constructively, has the best chance to maintain involved, happy, and responsible people.

Certainty

What does the future look like? Most people like a certain degree of predictability in that respect. We look for familiar patterns to make sense of our surroundings and to understand what is happening. Certainty leads to predictability, and it leads to a feeling of ease. Not knowing what will happen next leads to stress. In an unpredictable environment, we need to stay alert constantly to assess our chances of survival. Our brain never gets and gives the "all clear" signal in such an environment, and because of this, it cannot relax. In a secure, stable environment, it can.

Change is constant in today's society, as it is in the emerging Knowmad Society. Each day might bring a different work-space, different people, and different experiences. These dynamics put a great demand on people. Our hardware is not fully aligned with these developments. In traditional organizations, a lot of time is spent on planning, organizing, policies, structures, budgets, and forecasts. Working in these areas leads to a sense of security and control. However, they do not fit in knowmadic organizations where uncertainty and lack of predictability is the norm. What does it mean for the knowmadic worker? Can uncertainty be a certainty? Is it possible to relax in the certainty that things will be different in the morning? The next aspect, autonomy, might help us address these questions.

Autonomy

A sense of control over our circumstances leads to a release of dopamine. Autonomy is all about the ability to act, chose, and influence the situation. When we have a greater sense of autonomy, we are better able to deal with stressful situations. When there is little sense of autonomy, we feel like things are done to us, and not by us. In a knowmadic organization, the responsibility for decisions and outcomes lies with the worker, his- or herself. The knowmadic worker longs to create as much freedom of choice and as much influence as possible. In this respect, the knowmadic organization seems to encourage the release of dopamine. It's a better match to human biology than traditional organizations, where responsibility and freedom of choice often seem to get lost in a maze of rules and regulations that aim to create certainty.

Relatedness

Imagine three people in a virtual ball-tossing game. Only one of them, the subject, is actually playing the game, the other two are generated and controlled by the software of the game. The subject does not know this and thinks he is playing with two other people. Suddenly, the other two stop throwing the ball at the subject. They only toss the ball to each other and don't seem to notice the subject. The neural alarm system goes off, and just like in situations involving physical pain, disgusting odors or too much noise, the dorsal anterior cingulate cortex (dACC) is activated (Eisenberger et al, 2003). We like to be part of a group, and cooperation makes us feel good.

From an evolutionary point of view, the function of the alarm system is obvious: being part of the group drastically improves our chances for survival.

Knowmadic workers are not devoted to traditional group membership; their definition of the group is a different one than in traditional organizations. They relate to each other on shared values, areas of interest, and the exchange of knowledge. Face to face contact is combined with virtual contact. Geographic or organizational boundaries disappear. The group is not limited to a department, an organization, a city, or a country. The same goes for the boundary between work life and personal life. Friends and family are part of the network the knowmadic worker uses to "get things done."

Fairness

Getting a fair share of whatever there is to divide among group members leads to a release of dopamine. As should be clear by what we have written before, every signal that shows that we are a well-respected part of the group does the same. When we don't get a fair share, but we can explain it away as a function of effort or experience, we might still perceive an unequal share as fair. The more transparency about rewards, results, and arguments for both parties, the better we can assess whether our share is fair.

The sense of fairness is not only important when we, ourselves, are the subjects. Our brain also reacts when we experience unfairness in the world we live in. This might be an explanation for our sense of pleasure when we "do good" by doing volunteer work or fighting injustice in any way.

Motivators

So, the stress and reward system in our brain motivates us to take some kind of action. By experiencing hunger, we start looking for food. By burning ourselves, we step away from the fire. By experiencing the cold, we look for shelter. We see the same causality in social interaction. Feeling the pain of social exclusion can motivate us to start looking for a group to relate to. Because we experience grief over losing someone, we are eager to look after our loved ones; by working together we improve the position of the group.

Besides being a motivator for action, the stress and reward system might also work as a distraction. When we feel stressed because we experience a low status, are uncertain about the future, lack autonomy to change things, feel suspicious about our "fair share" and/ or we feel excluded from the group, our main attention will be focused on survival. This may not necessarily lead to trying to be a better group member, but could lead to getting set in our ways (creating predictability), defending our territory (holding on to autonomy),

political games (enhancing status), gossiping (checking our suspicions, working on relatedness), etc. By creating a respectful, safe, empowering, challenging-but-not-threatening environment, there will be a lot of energy and attention available for *creating* instead of *surviving*.

It seems obvious what this means for a work environment. How do the five factors of social interaction, to which the brain responds with stress or reward, influence the way we organize ourselves in Knowmad Society?

Practical dilemmas

In the previous part, we posed three questions:

- Can rules be formulated for the self-organization of people? What basic principles would we have to obey to come to an efficient and successful cooperation?
- Can we design the context or structure of an organization in a way that every individual is encouraged to take on leadership and followership, depending on which is best for the situation and task at hand?
- How do the factors of social interaction to which the brain responds with stress or reward (SCARF) influence the way we organize ourselves in Knowmad Society?

The next part of this chapter describes several examples of organizations that have successfully introduced new ways of organization (as a verb, not a noun). We look at what they do differently, how they do it, and at the impact on the people who work there. At the end of this chapter, we will revisit the above-mentioned questions and give our answers from a theoretical and practical perspective.

Knowmadic organizations

Humans organize themselves to co-exist, co-create, and achieve goals. This does not just apply to social environments. In order to survive, companies need to organize, too. During the last 100 years, the scientific management philosophy of Frederick Taylor became the leading viewpoint in the design of the operating systems of companies. The focus of his approach was on analyzing workflows and improving efficiency. Attention to the human element grew over the years and changed the perspective on an employee's contribution to the company. However, the hierarchical way of thinking mainly remained intact. Due to the challenges of mounting complexity and rapid change, as Kotter (2012) reveals in his article *Accelerate!*, there is now a need to let go of this hierarchical way of thinking. Enablers became disablers.

By using examples and experiences, we will show you the way to non-hierarchical modes of organization. We apply one credo: *Let the non-believers step aside of the way of the ones who have already adapted to it.*

In our line of work, we often meet managers and entrepreneurs who think it is impossible to change a hierarchical organization into a self-organizing network. It is generally accepted that approximately 75% of all change projects fail. Cultural and behavioral aspects seem to play a significant part in causing these failures. When asked, these leaders tell us that it has to do with difficulties they have experienced in the past with change management projects and with what they have read about others' experiences. Other times, leaders are critical of self-organizing because it might mean they lose their position of power. Thirdly, they point out their past experiences and how self-organizing has been tried and failed to succeed, like with Volvo in Sweden in the 1970s. Change seems difficult, and self-organization is, for most of them, a completely new perspective on organizing from which they might therefore shy away.

Context determines behavior

A relatively new Dutch home care organization was formed, called Buurtzorg Nederland. The company consists of self-organized teams of about 12 employees. Customer satisfaction is significantly higher than in similar organizations, and they report a growth in their efficiency rate of 30% in comparison to other home care companies. In 2011, their employee satisfaction was the highest amongst all large Dutch companies. In 2012, they received the "Best Employer Award" out of 269 participating companies, awarded by Effectory.

In the last 15 years, Buurtzorg Nederland has grown into an organization with 5,000 employees (Kuiken, 2010). Many of these workers came from traditional organizations, where change is considered difficult, and where bureaucracy and hierarchical structures were thought to be necessary to properly organize the business. One day, they quit their jobs and joined Buurtzorg Nederland! When they started at the company, those same people proved to be able to manage themselves successfully. How is this possible if human behavior is so difficult to change? Is Jos de Blok, the founder of Buurtzorg Nederland, just a lucky guy? On the other hand, does he have a very strict employee selection policy? Considering the number of employees, how has he reached this success?

We can answer those questions by looking at another, similar transition. This occurs when people move from being an employee to establishing him- or herself as an independent professional. Entrepreneurship triggers these individuals to instantly change their attitudes and behaviors. The returning theme in both examples is that the context in which people work largely determines their behavior. Culture (collective behavior) follows structure. It makes tinkering with people –a billion dollar industry– a hopeless exercise. Especially when the context in which these people work remains unchanged. Different behavior and a new culture require a fundamentally different context. Let us explore some patterns.

Organizing is a tool

The main reason why transitions in organizations do not work is that tools get confused with goals. Organizations, and especially hierarchical organizations, are often seen as the main goal itself. Institutions, whether being a department or a team within an organization or an organization as a whole, often pursue primarily one goal: the survival of the institution itself. The fallacy here, in our opinion, is that organizations are perceived as a static object, while, in fact, they are snapshots of a dynamic process called *organizing*. Organizations are solidified moments of organizing. When we elevate maintaining a temporary solidification of organizing to a goal itself, we are using our energy the wrong way. We deny the dynamic nature of reality. In this phenomenon, many organizations lose a lot of money, time, and energy.

This can easily be overcome. First, we need to become aware that every organization is solidified organizing. The present form of any organization is chosen in the past to co-exist, co-learn, and pursue certain goals. Only when we have a clear idea of how we like to co-exist and co-create, and which goals we wish to pursue, can we evaluate the current method of organizing for effectiveness. Second, we need to dare ask the "why" question when confronted with organizational aspects that are perceived as common sense. *Why* do we organize? Which goals do we pursue through our organizing? More importantly, we need to dare answer this question in all honesty and refuse to accept answers like, "that's just the way we do things around here," or, "we've tried everything and this is the best way by far."

The bottom line: It is always about cultivating behavior

By structuring, we want to cultivate behavior. Why? The right behavior of employees leads to success. It is that simple. Therefore, it is important for organizations to be very specific in the kind of behavior that they need from employees to be successful. Once this is clear, it is important to discover what structures cultivate that behavior. Looking at job advertisements, it seems in almost every organization innovative, entrepreneurial, involved, hands-on, pro-active, and socially skillful behavior is the desired behavior. However, the structures of those organizations usually do not cultivate it. On the contrary, they usually provoke standardized, bureaucratic, and solitary behavior.

New perspective, new perception

Another condition, for a successful transition to a non-hierarchical organization is to become aware of, and reconsider, the implicit assumptions driving organizational choices. Fundamental organizational change will only succeed if the basic assumptions driving organizing actually change. Change programs often fail because they start from the same, basic assumptions that have contributed to the need for change. That is doomed to fail! As Einstein is attributed to have said, "the significant problems we have cannot be solved at the same level of thinking with which we have created them."

The mainstream, commonly accepted view on organizing stems from the Newtonian worldview. That is, the world is made up of separate parts (i.e. molecules) that can be connected and used as building blocks. We call this a linear-mechanical approach to organizing. So, organizations are machines that can be built, rebuilt, used, traded, and repaired as such. Social Darwinism added the idea that these loose particles are in a constant battle – or fear of battle – with each other. This battle is the basis of and justification for our short-term profit maximization strategies in corporations (Coolpolitics, 2012).

The combination of both phenomena, separate building blocks in a constant battle for survival, is the basis of the prosperity that we are all experiencing. "The increasing dynamics and complexities, however, expose the Achilles heel of these systems," said Herman Wijffels, former director of the World Bank and former CEO of Rabobank. "The systems that previously guaranteed our success are the cause of the different crises we are currently experiencing. The need to fundamentally organize our organizations differently knocks hard at our doors" (Coolpolitics, 2012).

Fortunately, the "new" physics offer a new perspective. By analogy, Einsteinian and quantum physics teaches us that molecules are not the basic building blocks of our existence, but that we are all components of, and connected by, communication. Adopting that notion leads to a totally different way of looking at companies. They are complex systems instead of a linear production line of services or goods. Again, combined with the notion of "the survival of the fittest" (as in "best fitted for the circumstances") by Charles Darwin, an entirely new perspective on organizing arises. This fundamentally different way of organizing starts from the idea that organizations and their environments are interdependent and that system processes are cyclical rather than linear. This means that we can only evaluate organizations as a whole within their context and that it is useless to look at any separate part.

This sounds abstract. but we must start from abstraction to ensure that we begin with the correct principles and assumptions. When we do not, there is a risk that we are,what the English say, "rearranging the deck chairs on the Titanic." That is, we are busy with cosmetic issues while the company sinks. For the last 150 years, under the influence of the industrial revolution, we have perceived and treated businesses as mechanical systems. As previously mentioned, hierarchical organizations contributed a lot to the prosperity we have built, but they no longer deliver the desired results in the complex 21st century. In fact, as we will explain later, the systems that guaranteed success in the 20th century are counter-productive today.

A fundamentally different way

Besides Buurtzorg Nederland, there are more very interesting examples of businesses that organize themselves in a fundamentally different way. Take Finext, a financial services provider that is growing in times of financial crises. Finext shows extraordinary profit figures and is a magnet for talent. In May 2011, 85% of the employees joined in buying out all shares of Finext

from its parent company, Ordina. This is the first employee buyout in The Netherlands.

Another company, WDM, also defies the norms of the hierarchical organization. WDM rents, maintains, and repairs trucks. The company went bankrupt in late 2010. They restarted with new shareholders in early 2011. WDM ended the year of 2011 with a modest profit. For 2012, it looks like WDM will report a profitable year. In fact, the expected profit is higher than ever before. And, this will be achieved with one-third of the previous workforce. Moreover, the company does not have any managers – the employees lead the organization jointly.

First, we will examine the patterns behind the success of WDM, Finext and Buurtzorg Nederland. Then we will explore the specific situations of the three companies. Finally, we will discuss the transition process of letting go of hierarchies in formal organizations. Separation of form and function creates space.

An important first step in the de-hierarching process is to disconnect function and form. When we use the word "organization," nearly everyone thinks about organizations as a matrix or hierarchy. Remember, organization is solidified organizing. Organizing is a process of structuring work to realize efficiency and effectiveness. As stated earlier, organizing is a tool and not a goal in itself. It is essential to put function before form. Legitimate functional questions that lie at the basis of the organizational choices are:

1   What behaviors of employees are needed to excel in achieving our organizational goals?
2   What structures support these behaviors the best? And, to break the barriers of the existing organization:
3   How would we structure our organization if we founded it today?

A practical example is the recurring discussion about trust and control. Advocates of trust-based organizing, experience the command and control structure of the hierarchical organization as oppressive, bureaucratic, and ineffective. Opponents state that it is naïve to organize based on trust. There are countless examples where employees abuse trust, and it leads to chaos, theft, and inefficiency.

When we transcend the polarity and look at the functions of control and trust, it is conceivable that a structure can be created in which the starting point is trust. By applying transparency, a corrective environment may be created so the naïve aspect is covered without spiraling into in a bureaucratic-hierarchical reflex.

This is illustrated in a real life example. At Finext, employees hand their expense statement declarations to the back office, and, without control, the declared amount is credited directly to their bank account. The only condition is that the statement is visible for everyone on the company intranet.

It is good to realize that any form of organizing is a tool to achieve goals. What purpose is served with a hierarchical organization? Or, what is its function? Hierarchical organization is a tool to create efficient manufacturing processes. It is a tool to utilize resources efficiently and to make output manageable. However, organizing hierarchically has a number of unintended side effects. The most common side effects are:

1   It averages 50-60% utilization of the potential of employees (see Managers Online, 2011) – well-organized mediocrity.
2   Lack of innovative strength, adaptability, and agility.

3 Takes responsibility away from people and encourages docility. This cultivates learned helplessness – organized irresponsibility.

4 Focus on separated (partial) interests., and lost sight of the importance of the bigger picture and their own influence on it – an "us vs. them" culture.

These side effects are acceptable if the work is simple and repetitive and the business functions in a predictable, stable environment. In a complex and dynamic environment, though, the influence of the unintended consequences of organizing hierarchically is unacceptably high. It is good to become aware that hierarchical organization is a form of organizing. The separation of function and form provides space. Space to find and apply better working alternatives, given the setting.

How context determines behavior

So, if innovative, entrepreneurial, involved, hands-on, pro-active, and socially skilful behavior is the right approach in most organizations, and the employees of Buurtzorg Nederland, Finext, and WDM do behave that way, what can we learn from their organizational choices? What are the common denominators? In medication, we talk about "active ingredients." They are the substances that cause the desired effect of the drug. What are the active ingredients in de-hierarchization? Here's a summary:

1 **Values driven.** Value based principles provide a foundation and compass in the process of de-hierarchization. Hierarchical organizations are rule-based. The advantage of principle-based organizing is that principles give direction for behavioral choices in every situation. Rules are rigid and blind to reality. Principles allow for using one's own brain. Rules enforce docility. Principles spur people to take responsibility. Employees who take responsibility help organizations excel. Examples of Finext's values are: Doing the work you love; Trust the ones you work with; And, no rules or politics.

2 **Value networks.** De-hierarchic organizations structure themselves as value networks. They see and organize themselves as an interdependent system that is inextricably linked and mutually dependent on their environment. They seek synergy with all stakeholders and mutual value creation beyond short-term profit maximization. They think and act in a way that serves value

creation for all stakeholders. With each choice, the impact on all stakeholders is considered. This focus on value creation and interconnectivity appeals to the need for meaning among employees. Talented individuals like to work in value networks (van den Hoff, 2011).

3 Organically structured as

small in large, and small and agile entrepreneurial elements in a connected network. This combines the advantages of being small with the advantages of the larger organization (Wintzen, 2007). Key ingredients for this type of network organization are:

1   The system and environment is complex;
2   Rapid interaction between the components of the system (communication);
3   Learning based on feedback (local information);
4   Delegation of processes that can be regulated better at lower levels; and,
5   Timely escalation of issues that must be solved "higher" in the system, after which they are delegated.

As mentioned above, Buurtzorg Nederland works in small teams of 12 people. Finext works with teams called Business Projects, which also comprise 12 people. The teams are profit and loss responsible, and they make their own strategic, tactical, and operational choices.

4 Passion and talent go before

structure. Structure is the stage on which talent & passion excel. Structure is serving and will be updated if it does not have added value anymore. In network organizations, committed employees work with passion and talents on projects. The "chore" tasks the group members divide among themselves are based on a deep understanding that these also need to be done. The big advantage is that intrinsic motivation is the driving force for employees. Second, it keeps everyone aware of the necessity of those tasks. If they are no longer needed, they are no longer done, instead of maintaining them out of habit, or because someone was hired to do them and wants to hang on to the job. The self-determination theory by Deci & Ryan (2000) identifies three innate needs that, if satisfied, allow optimal functioning and growth:

• Competence
• Relatedness
• Autonomy

Network organizations provide an environment that meets these needs. Thus, the potential of employees can be reached. Talented people like to work in an environment in which they can excel.

5   Shard leadership. In all three organizations, there is no imposed hierarchy. Power is decentralized explicitly. Leadership is a task for everyone. Leaders in a network are leaders by the grace of their followers. The best person, given the present issue, is taking the lead. Shared leadership departs from equivalence and allows, where necessary, hierarchy to occur naturally. This creates servant leadership and discards it of all its frills, ego, and status, which is a lot more functional. Thus, craftsmanship becomes the focus again. And, you avoid the Peter Principle: "In a hierarchy, every employee tends to rise to his level of incompetence" (Peter, L. L. & Hull, 1969).

6   Transparency. In a network, information is shared. So, fast-paced information exchange is encouraged. Information is generated and used locally. Thus, organizations are closely related to their customers, and they can respond to change quickly. Transparency of information is a prerequisite for:

- Local entrepreneurship: Having the correct information to be able to adequately respond to situations and opportunities that arise in support

of the larger picture.
- A corrective environment: Visibility contributes to a moral compass for employees. In the possible absence of self-discipline, or when possibly erroneous decisions occur, the environment through transparency can quickly adjust matters. This creates short and powerful learning loops.

7   Cyclical processes. The command and control structure is typical for hierarchical systems. Input leads are set via a structured and manageable process to a predictable output. Growth is linear and something which one can manufacture. Need a new budget? Last year + 5%.

A network organization starts from cyclical processes. Often, budgets are serving instead of leading because there is not much predictability when it comes to a dynamic environment. It is important to be alert and well informed in order to respond to developments. Ambitions and expectations are aligned and regularly validated and/or adjusted. With a keen eye on reality, the highest achievable objective is pursued. In hierarchical systems, the objective is often elevated as being a goal in itself instead of reaching as high as possible.

Time and energy is spent on keeping goals "realistic," and on justifying why targets are not met.

In addition, there is continuous attention to the impact of the organization on its environment. Cyclical processes are much more sustainable and don't produce large heaps of waste.

8   Democratization. Hierarchies are centralized and autocratic. This leads to a lack of agility and capacity for change. De-hierarchization brings decentralization of authority and responsibility. De-hierarchization leads to democratization, which organizes authority and responsibility as close to the customer as possible. Therefore, employees can respond in an adequate and entrepreneurial way to customer demands and change.

De-hierarchization in practice

So far, we have described the changing expectations and needs in today's work life, we have looked at human behavior in social processes, and we have described some of the common denominators of businesses that are well adjusted to Knowmadic Society. Now, let's have a closer look at those organizations to give an idea of their organizational form at this time.

Buurtzorg Nederland revisited

Buurtzorg Nederland, as described earlier, is a home care organization with 5,000 employees. The organization was founded in 2006 by Jos de Blok, a former manager at a "normal" home care organization. Buurtzorg delivers the prescribed care in 37.75 percent of the indicated hours where comparable organizations need 70 percent of the indicated hours. Their client satisfaction rate is 8.7 on a scale from 0 to 10 (Nivel figures) and is the highest in the sector. Their overhead costs are 10% (average in Home care is about 30%). In 2011, Buurtzorg had the highest employee satisfaction of large businesses in The Netherlands. In 2009, they realized a growth of 3,684%. It is an impressive performance record, right?

By letting teams of 12 highly skilled nurses provide care, and organizing nurses in small autonomous care teams, the resolving power and professionalism of staff is fully used. Supported by coaches of the national organization, the teams are profit and loss responsible. The coaches have no power, and so they can only advise and coach.

These neighborhood care teams are supported by a national organization. It uses modern ICT applications, thus reducing administrative costs to a minimum. The cost of management and overhead is kept as limited as possible. In short: better care at a lower cost is an attractive proposition for clients, professionals, and insurers.

Jos de Blok came up with this structure by asking himself what home care is about. He came to the conclusion that home care is about helping clients, as quickly as possible, to take care of themselves (what you do not use, you lose), and that clients want to be helped as much as possible by the same professional. Due to the small, smartly organized overhead cost, autonomy for professionals, and the appeal that the organization is doing on the organizational ability and common sense of employees, professionals like to work for the company. As mentioned earlier, it is striking that employees who come from mainstream organizations perform much better, with much more pleasure, and with more satisfaction while working for Buurtzorg Nederland. People do what they love and what they were trained for, instead of spending most of their time tending to bureaucratic procedures.

Finext

Finext unburdens the CFOs of the 500 largest Dutch companies or foreign businesses headquartered in The Netherlands of many business services. The company has about 120 employees. The employee satisfaction rate was in three consecutive years, 8.1, 8.3 and 8.5. (on a scale from 0 to 10) where similar companies score an average of 7.0. The staff involvement is 80% versus 20% at comparable companies. The employee absentee rate has been below 2% for years now. They were, by far, the best performing child company of the Ordina Group, and their customer satisfaction is significantly higher than in similar organizations.

Finext originated in the Vision Web, a network organization with two activities: change management and ICT. services The Vision Web has quickly grown into an organization with 600 employees. In 2003, the Ordina bought the Vision Web. Until 2011, Finext operated autonomously under as an Ordina holding, but in May of that year, 85% of the employees bought the shares of Finext. This was the first successful employee buyout in The Netherlands.

What brings success?

Finext's success stems from the way it is organized. The company is a network of profit and loss responsible business projects. The projects are built around a specific service instance, a geographic location, or another common denominator. Employees, now intrapreneurs, commit themselves, based on passion and talent, to one or more projects. All information is shared transparently, from knowledge, insights, and leads, as well as salary and customer data. This makes Finext a dynamic and entrepreneurial breeding ground where everyone feels responsible for the success of the company.

There are no job titles within Finext. This literally means that there are no managers or staff officers. Everyone works on billable projects for clients. In addition, the employees all take part in the organizational tasks to manage the company, based on their competence and interest. These include recruitment, organizing client events, internal auditing, strategic choices, etc. Decisions are taken at the level of impact of the decision, preferably as close as possible to the customer. Anyone who may be impacted by the decision has the opportunity to be part of the decision making process. Sometimes this way of decision making takes more time than autocratic decision making. Nevertheless, as Fokke Wijnstra, one of the founders of Vision Web, and still closely involved in Finext says, "sometimes you have to take the time to speed up."

The "extra" time that is spent on the decision-making process is dwarfed by the time saved in the implementation of those resolutions. If you consider the "implementation time" in autocratic decision-making regimes, it is the complete process of having the discussion about the decision and implementing it that takes far more time. This makes the internal organization of Finext up to 30% less costly and more efficient than similar companies. Let us take their administration as an example. It employs 2.4 FTE, and provides the overall administration plus the payroll in house. In addition, they earn back their salary costs because they also engage in project work for other companies. That is what we call real intrapreneurship!

Adaptability: A matter of survival

"Well," we hear entrepreneurs often object when we talk with them about the de-hierarchization of their companies: "If I could start again, I would like to build a network company, but I already have an existing organization and changing it into a network organization will never succeed."

Adaptability is the most valuable skill that exists. Charles Darwin made it clear with his "survival of the fittest" theory. Companies which are not able to adapt to the changing environment will not survive. It is that simple. Right, change sometimes hurts. But, that is nothing compared to the "pain" which occurs when companies structurally fail to adapt.

For the transition process of de-hierarchization, we see two basic strategies.

First,
start your company
next door

"Large, hierarchical companies are often destined for the same fate as the dinosaur: extinction by a chronic lack of adaptability." These are the words of the late Eckart Winzten, the entrepreneur behind BSO, now known as Atos Origin. During his career, he built BSO from 10 to 10,000 employees. It was his strategy to split up his company in two separate organizations when it reached the size of 50 employees. What can you learn from Winzten's strategy when your company grows bigger then 50 employees, and changing the company becomes very difficult? Do not beat a dead horse, but just restart next door. Keep working hierarchically in the existing company. Invent and build a new company parallel to it with a number of crazy pioneers.

Second,
shift radically from the
existing organization
to a new context

Build, with a core team, a new de-hierarchical organizational context for a business or organization in a short period –up to two months. Pick a start date, and run your company in the new context from day one. We applied this kind of organizational transition and found out that it works both in production environments as well in knowledge-intensive companies. Examples we worked on include the car rental company, WDM, and a section of a medium-sized engineering company. Employees, apart from a few exceptions, soon picked up their new roles and behaviors. We now literally see that creating a new context develops new behavior, just as what happened with nurses from a regular company migrating to Buurtzorg Nederland. If the context is correct, the desired behavior follows.

Finally,

Back to the practical dilemmas. Earlier, we have posed three questions. Now it is time for some answers, based on the practical and theoretical information we shared in this chapter.

Can rules be formulated for the self-orga-nization of people? What basic principles would we have to obey to come to an efficient and successful cooperation?

If we summarize this chapter in a few simple rules for self-organization, then these would most likely be:

- Agree on/review what you want to achieve by coming together as a group of individuals;
- Agree on/review what value system you want to maintain getting there, and how this translates to behavior;
- Create transparency in information that is vital to the achievement of goals and to the maintenance of the value system so that all members have access to this information at all times;
- Stay away from solidified organiza-tion and positions, hierarchical or otherwise;
- Always question or allow questions on why things are done a certain way;
- Check regularly whether what you are doing makes you happy and act upon it; and,
- Check regularly whether you would rather do something else and act upon it.

Can we design the context or structure of an organization in a way that every

individual is encouraged to take on leadership and followership, depending on which is best for the situation and task at hand?

The enablers of the 20th century are the disablers of the 21st century. John Kotter (2012) wrote, "although traditional hierarchies and processes - which together form a company's 'operating system' - are optimized for day-to-day business, they can't handle the challenges of mounting complexity and rapid change." Why? The patterns and operating systems of hierarchical organizations preach mediocrity, obedience, and docility. This behavior was necessary to optimize day-to-day business in the industrial era. The mounting complexity and rapid change explains the necessity to design struc-tures that encourages workers to take the responsibility to lead in their field of expertise and level of competence. Organic structures decentralize power. The democratization of organizations leads to safe environments where workers feel ownership for the compa-nies' interests.

This leads to adaptive behavior; the best-qualified person for the current task takes the lead, and the others follow. Biologically, it satisfies basic needs such as status and safety. And, it enhances status because workers are a valued part of the team. It is safer because, on topics where workers are less competent, others can take the lead.

How do the factors of social interaction to which the brain responses with stress or reward (SCARF) influence the way we organize ourselves in Knowmad Society?

We argue self-organizing environments satisfy the basic biological needs to which the brain responses far better than hierarchical environments. The lack of hierarchy influences the sense of status in a positive way, as does the appreciation of different talents and passions. There is no more or no less certainty as in a traditional organization, and no effort is put in pretending to be able to create it. Workers are very autonomous, they can act and influence any situation, although that doesn't mean they will always get their way! Relationships pose the same challenge as in traditional organizations. However, since there is no leader, there is no person designated to deal with differences and conflict. If people want to work on their relationships, it is up to them. When it comes to relatedness, the feeling of belonging to a group, self-organizing environments show

potential for great cohesion. This has to do with the common values that bind people together within an organization. Workers are usually very committed and very connected in these companies. And, for the element of fairness: because all information is readily available, it is easy for people to check whether they got their fair share. If they did not, all they have to do is change it – and explain why to their colleagues.

We will not pretend the sun always shines in these companies. It is hard work to have honest and open discussions about values, about behavior, and about decisions. It is not always easy to take total responsibility for one's behavior and results. And, one person is better than the other at vocalizing his or her needs and troubles. But, observing the behavior of workers in a self-organizing environment drives our conclusions. The goals workers achieve, the commitment they show, and, above all, the fun they have, leaves no other conclusion.

Do you want to adapt to Knowmad Society? Do not change people; change the companies they work for.

REFERENCES

Coolpolitics. (2012). Lowlands University 2012 - Herman Wijffels, from vimeo.com/47764053

Eisenberger, N. I., Lieberman, M D., & Williams, K. D. (2003). Does Rejection Hurt? An fMRI Study of Social Exclusion. *Science, 302*(5643), 290-292.

van den Hoff, R. (2011). *Society 3.0.* Utrecht: Stichting Society 3.0.

Kotter, J. P. (2012). Accelerate! *Harvard Business Review, 90*(11). Retrieved from www.awberymanagement.co.uk/resources/files/john_kotter_accelerate.pdf

Krause, J., Ruxton, G.D. & Krause, S. (2009). Swarm intelligence in animals and humans. *Trends in Ecology & Evolution, 25* (1), 28-34.

Kuiken, B. (2010). *De laatste manager.* Uitgeverij Haystack.

Managers Online. (2011). Onderbenutting arbeidspotentieel ondermijnt economische groei. Retrieved from www.managersonline.nl/nieuws/11648/onderbenutting-arbeidspotentieel-ondermijnt-economische-groei.html

Nuytten, D. (2011). *Geluk zit in je hoofd.* Uitgeverij Vrijdag: Antwerpen.

Peter, L. L. & Hull, R. (1983). *Het Peterprincipe, waarom alles altijd verkeerd gaat, Engelse versie.* L.J. Veen BV, Utrecht.

Peters, T. J. & Waterman, R. H. (1982). *In search of excellence: Lessons from America's best-run companies.* New York: Free Press.

Ratey, J. J. (2008). *Spark: The revolutionary new science of exercise and the brain.* Hachette Book Group, New York.

Reynolds, C. (2001). Boids (Flocks, herds, and schools: A distributed behavioral model). Retrieved from www.red3d.com/cwr/boids/

Robson, D. (2011). A brief history of the brain. *NewScientist, 211,* 40-45.

Rock, D. (2008). SCARF: A brain-based model for collaborating with and influencing others. *NeuroLeadership Journal, 1*(1), 44 – 52.

Ryan, R. M. & Deci, E. L. (2000). Self-determination theory and the facilitation of intrinsic motivation, social development and well-being. *American Psychologist, 55*(1), 68-78.

Schutter, D. & den Boer, J. (2008). Emoties. Van subjectieve ervaring naar neurale circuits.. In F. Wijnen & F. Verstraten (Eds), *Het brein te kijk.* (p. 155-183). Amsterdam: Pearson.

VDM. (2010). *Fatale en vitale spiralen in de zorg: 16 zorgeigen oplossingen Jaap van der Mei.* Utrecht: VDM Projects.

van Vugt, M. & Ahuja, A. (2011). *De natuurlijke leider.* Utrecht: Bruna Uitgevers.

Wijnstra, F. (2012). Publicaties. Retrieved from www.fokkewijnstra.nl/Publicaties.html

Williams, L.M., Liddell, B.J., Kemp, A.H., Bryant, R.A., Meares, R.A., Peduto, A.S. et al. (2006). Amygdala-prefrontal dissociation of subliminal and supraliminal fear. *Human Brain Mapping, 27,* 652-661.

Wintzen, E. (2007). *Eckart's notes.* Lemniscaat.

notes

Glue additional info
on this page

notes

....

....

....

....

....

....

....

....

....

....

and on this one

....

....

....

....

notes

and here

notes

and here too

Relationships as the ultimate pedagogy: Making everyone a life-long teacher

BY CHRISTINE RENAUD

"TO TEACH IS TO LEARN TWICE."

Neal Whitman

'THE MAGIC OF PEER LEARNING IS THAT YOU DO NOT NEED TO GET A DEGREE TO BECOME A TEACHER. ONE JUST HAS TO LIVE.'

'SHARING KNOWLEDGE WITH KNOWN OR NEW PEERS PROVIDES A CONTEXT WHERE NEW INTIMACIES MAY BE CREATED, BROADENING OUR SENSE OF BELONGING WITHIN A LOCAL OR WIDER COMMUNITY.'

CHRISTINE RENAUD

'WE NEED TO RECOGNIZE THE POTENTIAL CONTRIBUTION OF OUR PEERS AS FLEXIBLE, RELEVANT, AND KNOWLEDGEABLE LIFE-LONG TEACHERS.'

'MANY USERS ARE BLOWN AWAY AFTER THEIR FIRST MEETING, AS IT IS OFTEN THE FIRST TIME THAT THEY TAKE AN INTENTIONAL STAND FOR THEIR OWN EDUCATION.'

SUMMARY

RELATIONSHIPS AS THE ULTIMATE PEDAGOGY:
MAKING EVERYONE A LIFE-LONG TEACHER
- Christine Renaud -

As a podcast producer in New York City in 2008, I got to spend more and more time on emerging social networks such as Facebook and Twitter. I noticed from many posts that I was not the only one who learned from the people who surrounded me: *Hey, can someone help me with Photoshop tonight? Got a deadline for tomorrow and just can't seem to make it work. Will pay for beer(s).*

As a trained educator and social entrepreneur, that got me thinking. It is neither actually the schools I attended nor the curriculum I followed that led me so far from what my life could have been: it's the amazing people I met throughout my journey that trained and transformed me. Three years later, our venture, E-180 was born. It is a matchmaking website connecting like-minded folks interested in sharing a coffee in person to learn something new or share their knowledge with others. The idea is to take social networking a step further: we connect people on the basis of their learning needs and available skills to foster in person, one-hour long micro-mentoring sessions.

Our ultimate goal is to unveil all the knowledge our communities' life-long teachers hold secretly. Because we believe spaces play an incredible hub-like role, bringing people together who have compatible knowledge needs, we are now slowly working ourselves into all places where humans gather: coffee shops, conferences, libraries, museum, offices, airplanes, and so on. With the proper structure and recognition, peer learning holds a key to enriching, timely, and personalized education for us all.

Renting a stranger's house on the other side of the world, sharing an office space with fellow self-employed creatives, finding out about breaking news before the journalists themselves: often without knowing it, many 21st century citizens now lead a life that has been deeply impacted by the open Web and its values of collaboration. A new awareness of our interdependence transforms the way we consume, work, and travel.

Learning is also profoundly transformed by this novel global proximity. But while many educators and technology entrepreneurs are redefining classroom standards, few initiatives, both inside and outside schools, question the very dogma on which our educational institutions are built: The very concept of education being anything else than the broadcasting of information from one to many. The expert (ex-peer) still acts as a knowledge broadcaster while participants are confined to the role of silent spectators.

Knowmads work for constant innovation in a world where problems and solutions are created everyday. Their reality calls for an adaptable, personalized education option that simply cannot be provided solely by the current broadcast-based education model. What is the missing link that will contribute in delivering the "just-in-time" education our knowmadic society requires? We think it is peer learning. Moreover:

We need to recognize the potential contribution of our peers as flexible, relevant and knowledgeable life-long teachers.

How does peer learning compare with broadcasted education? And what is the structure needed to scale peer learning? In my investigation, some answers to these questions were found in the visionary work of education pioneer Ivan Illich, while some were pulled from the inspiring work of my own peers at the Mozilla Foundation, Skillshar,e and Meetup. Many more answers (and an exponentially growing amount of questions) were inducted by our members in the experiment my team and I have been conducting at E-180, a matchmaking site that connects like-minded people interested in sharing knowledge one-on-one, over a coffee.

So here is it all, from one educator to another, from peer to peer.

To teach is to learn twice

The first published reports of students teaching students in higher education began to appear in the 1960s. The motivation was, guess what, "dissatisfaction of faculty with large lecture courses in which students played a passive role." The answer to this discomfort was found in peer-assisted learning, defined by Topping and Ehly (1998) as, "the acquisition of knowledge and skill through active helping and supporting among status equals or matched companions" (p. 1)

As peer learning began to build steam within the educational system, research showed that the benefits of peer learning were found both with peer teachers and peer learners. Moreover, "studies demonstrate that the cognitive processing used to study material to teach is different from studying to take a test and [that] peer learners benefit because of the ability of peers to teach at the right level" (Whitman, 1988, p. iii).

When reviewing the literature, we come across revealing titles such as *Peer learning in higher education: Learning from and with each other* or *Strategic uses of peer learning in children's education.* Could peer learning eventually detached itself from broadcasted education and become more than math tutoring, SAT preparation, or children's socialization in kindergarten? Yes, according to Ivan Illich in his self-explanatory titled essay, *Unschooling society.* The priest-turned-professor believed it could actually be the road for a complete redefinition of education:

> *Universal education through schooling is not feasible.*
> *It would be no more feasible if it were attempted by means of alternative institutions built on the style of present schools. Neither new attitudes of teachers toward their pupils nor the proliferation of educational hardware or software (in classroom or bedroom), nor finally the attempt to expand the pedagogue's responsibility until it engulfs his pupils' lifetimes will deliver universal education. The current search for new educational funnels must be reversed into the search for their institutional inverse: educational webs which heighten*

the opportunity for each one to transform each moment of his
living into one of learning, sharing, and caring. (Illich, 1971)

Teachers, leave them kids alone?

Apart from fostering a stronger engagement toward learning (which is, in itself, not too bad), what makes peer learning superior, or at least complementary, to broadcasted education?

Learning from Life itself

Peer learning allows us to learn from the lived experience of those around us, instead of cramming into our brains what Whitehead calls *inert knowledge*:

> *With good discipline, it is always possible to pump into the*
> *minds of a class a certain quantity of inert knowledge. [The*
> *rationale behind this action being that] the mind is an instru-*
> *ment, you first sharpen it, and then use it [...]. I don't know who*
> *was first responsible for this analogy of the mind to a dead*
> *instrument. [...] I have no hesitation in denouncing it as one*
> *of the most fatal, erroneous, and dangerous conceptions ever*
> *introduced into the theory of education. The mind is never pas-*
> *sive: it is a perpetual activity, delicate, receptive, responsive to*
> *stimulus. You cannot postpone its life until you have sharpened*
> *it. [...] There is only one subject-matter for education, and that*
> *is Life in all its manifestations. (Whitehead, 1967, p. 5)*

And, as learners, we naturally seize life everywhere it happens: at home with family and friends, in the studio with watercolors, a violin, or a yoga mat; as well as at work, with our colleagues, clients, stresses, and successes. So much, that peer learning is at times even known to be THE go-to approach for learning on-the-fly. According to the *New approaches to life-long learning* survey, over 56% of the Canadian workforce develops most of its competencies by discussing them informally with their peers (Livingstone, 2003).

Mobilizing lost gold

Have you ever thought about all the knowledge serving only one person because of a lack of the appropriate funnels directing it toward where many others would learn it? One could argue that all the information you need can already be found on the Internet, and that it provides the perfect receptacle for everything you want to share with the world. This is not so true, according to Paul King, visiting scholar at the Redwood Center for Theoretical Neuroscience at UC Berkeley:

> *...with 10,000 synapses per neuron and 10 billion neurons, one could reconstruct the memory state of the network with 10,000 * 10 billion = 100 terabytes. However, the actual memory capacity of the brain is probably quite a bit lower than that, and could be 100 gigabytes or less. If you were to write down "everything you know and remember", how many printed books could you fill? A 500 page book is about 1 MB. Could you fill 100 books (3 bookshelves)? That would only be 100 megabytes! (King, 2012)*

Given that a negligible percentage of us have codified the sums of our knowledge into hundreds of books, it is safe to say that what you share in a structured or unstructured discussion with a peer hasn't necessary yet been encompassed by the Web.

Strengthening our communities

Charles V. Willie (1994) writes, "we should keep what is good for everybody, and change what hurts one of us." That rings true when bonds are tight within the members of a community, and also when we actually can see and feel the impact of our actions on the life of others. Block (2008) sees small group settings as the ultimate unit of transformation for community building as, "the intimacy [...] provides the structure where people overcome isolation and where the experience of belonging is created."

Sharing knowledge with known or new peers provides a context where new intimacies may be created, broadening our sense of belonging within a local or wider community.

Individualizing learning

As UNESCO (2005) stated in a report on knowledge societies, Web 2.0 created an "unexpected flow of information [which] leads to a lack of people's control on their education [...]. According to some, half the information circulating is simply false or inaccurate."

When one wants to learn something, where should that person begin? How can one tell what is right from what might lead you down the wrong path? As life-long learners, we need to be oriented in order to take advantage of all the resources now available to learn outside of broadcasted education. Peer learning provides us with knowledge brokers, the trusted guides we need who are willing to accompany us through the process of learning something new and navigate the great amount of information available.

Making the invisible visible

However, two major obstacles still stand in the way of those motivated to meet and learn from their peers. First, there is a common misperception among adults that in order to pursue one's development, that person must go "back to school." This makes learning a heavy endeavor, where one has to hit "pause" on her life to pursue education. This, combined with the lack of recognition of informal learning, makes peer learning look more like a hobby than a valid form of education. As stated in a Mozilla working paper:

> *Most existing systems of educational degrees and job-relevant accreditation require enrollment in formal programs and institutions and dictate that learning needs to follow pre-scribed paths. Informal, peer-based and self-directed learning is only acknowledged to the degree that it supports the formal curriculum. (Mozilla Foundation and Peer 2 Peer University, 2012)*

Another obstacle is the difficulty, once out of school, of finding like-minded people willing to share their knowledge. Even if we are more connected than ever, most of our online connections remain superficial, and the commitment needed to maintain a relationship is low.

Creating the next webs

Let's get back to Illich, who saw in the late 1960s what is now influencing the work of hundreds of educational tech entrepreneurs. According to him, the redefinition of education was directly related to the necessity of helping serendipity emerge, using technology to connect people who share interests, and therefore create the learning webs we need to transform each moment into a learning one:

> *The operation of a peer-matching network would be simple. The user would identify himself by name and address and describe the activity for which he sought a peer. A computer would send him back the names and addresses of all those who had inserted the same description. It is amazing that such a simple utility has never been used on a broad scale for publicly valued activity. (Ivan Illich in Mozilla Foundation and Peer 2 Peer University, 2012)*

This call resonated, 40 years later, with some of the world's most successful tech entrepreneurs. The increasing standardization of the United States' educational system following No Child Left Behind generated a burst of interest and criticism of the schooling system, leading to an era of major educational innovation. Some educators emerged as intrapreneurs and decided to work the system from within; many decided, instead, to step aside and to use the Web to help people reclaim their education, far from standards and testing.

Some leaders emerged from this movement. Within a couple of months, Skillshare became the most popular online "marketplace of classes from teachers in your community," and Meetup provides the tools necessary for "groups of people with shared interests to plan meetings and form offline clubs in local communities around the world."

Recognizing and documenting informal learning

But as long as we can't "prove" or document the results of peer learning, its impact will still be considered peripheral and marginal to the structured system. That's the challenge tackled by the Mozilla Foundation, with its Open badge project:

Imagine [...] a world where your skills and competencies were captured more granularly across many different contexts, were collected and associated with your online identity and could be displayed to key stakeholders to demonstrate your capacities. In this ideal world, learning would be connected across formal and informal learning contexts, and you could discover relevant opportunities and craft your own learning pathways at your own pace, based on your own interests and learning styles. [...] The next step is to more systematically support and acknowledge this learning so that these skills and competencies are available and become part of the conversation in hiring decisions, school acceptances, mentoring opportunities and even self-evaluations. This is where badges come in." By offering an open API to their badge system framework to all organizations interested in contributing to their shareholders "badge backpack", the Mozilla Open badge project plays a crucial role in the "connected learning ecology by acting as a bridge between contexts and making these alternative learning channels, skills and types of learning more viable, portable and impactful".Community classes, learning groups, badge framework: what is still missing in this "learning ecosystem" to foster life-long peer learning and peer-teaching? The tools necessary to connect like-minded strangers interested in a more individualized learning experience, just like this one-on-one tutoring we find throughout schooling, but based on Life itself. (Mozilla Foundation and Peer 2 Peer University, 2012)

Introducing E-180: Not your typical matchmaking site

As a podcast producer in New York City in 2008, I got to spend more and more time on emerging social networks such as Facebook and Twitter. I noticed from many posts that I was not the only one who learned from the people who surrounded me: *Hey, can someone help me with Photoshop tonight? Got a deadline for tomorrow and just can't seem to make it work. Will pay for beer(s).*

As a trained educator and social entrepreneur, that got me thinking.

It is not actually the schools I attended or the curriculum I followed that led me so far from what my life could have been: it's the amazing people I met throughout my journey that trained and transformed me. The people we meet throughout our lives are like living, ever-evolving books: they might become our guides and follow us for the rest of our lives. If we take good enough care of them, they will allow us to go back to them to learn some more, or to relearn the things we might have forgotten as we go along. How could we replicate, optimize and scale those water cooler conversations? What could be the impact on our communities and businesses if we unveiled, with the help of social technologies, all the knowledge each one of us holds, and made it available, in the form of one-on-one, face-to-face, educational conversations between two people? What if we could make everyone a life-long teacher?

Three years later, E-180 was born. *It is a matchmaking website, connecting like-minded folks interested in sharing a coffee in person to learn something new or share their knowledge with others.* The idea is to take social networking a step further: we connect people on the basis of their learning needs and available skills, and foster in person, one hour-long micro-mentoring sessions.

After one year of private prototyping, in November 2012, we launched our public bilingual version to over 1,600 members, who generated over 300 in-person knowledge-sharing meetings during this first phase. From *how to live through loss: grieving through drawing* to *how to travel with less than $10 per day*, our members share their most intimate experiences and their most "out there" skills.

An example: The first E-180 meeting was held right after our private launch, between Élodie, who had never really traveled and wanted to go to India by herself for 4 months, and Paul, who had spent almost a year over there. Slightly nervous, they both met for lunch in an Indian restaurant and chatted about India, its people, flavors and transportation for two hours. Here is what Paul had to say about it, when he wrote about his experience on our blog:

> *We were so excited to get started once we met, we weren't even sure where to begin. The walk to our meeting place, "Parc-Ex," the Indian district of town, where we ate, gave us some time to get to know each other before diving into a conversation about chicken and curry recipes. That's where everything started.*
> *(Mariuzzo-Raynaud, 2012)*

After the meeting, Élodie traveled to India for 4 months, came back, and is now offering *how to travel to India as a single woman* on E-180. That's the magic of peer learning: no need to get a degree to become a teacher. One just has to live. "It completely changed my perception of my relationships and the impact they might have on my learning," said Élodie at the public, bilingual launch of E-180.

A year-long experiment in connecting knowmads

What did we learn from our year-long experiment in matchmaking for peer-learning? What are our remaining questions and where will we go from here?

- **People are humble.** Most of our users feel uncomfortable telling the world that they are good at something.

  Our question: How can we better help people identify what knowledge they can share with others around them?

- **People are generous, yet busy.** The driving factor behind people spending an hour with a fellow human is simply generosity. Yet, people are busy, which is their top excuse for not getting as involved as they would like to.

  Our question: Should we implement a system of rewards (open currency, points, open badges, etc.) to recognize the contributions of our outstanding members?

  Our question: Would public, individualized learning plans be an option to utilize the power of community accountability to keep our users on track in regard to their learning goals?

- **People feel inspired by peer learning.** Many users are blown away after their first meeting, as it is often the first time that they take an intentional stand for their own education.

  Our question: How can we measure success, in order to reproduce and scale it through our recommendation algorithm?

- **The need for peer learning is huge.** We see new opportunities for collaboration to enhance peer learning everyday.

  Our question: How can we create peer learning hubs in public spaces using mobile technologies?

And now what?

The observation of like-minded organizations as well as our experience at E-180 convinced us that, by inspiring people within a community and providing them with the tools they need to learn from one another, we contribute to the emergence of a society where the potential development of any individual does not exclusively rely on the broadcast of information. We facilitate the formation of links of interdependence which can be created among the members of a community.

What will be our ongoing contribution to this rising movement? Our ultimate goal is to unveil all the knowledge our communities' life-long teachers hold secretly. And, because we believe spaces play an incredible hub-like role, bringing people together who have compatible knowledge needs, we are now slowly working ourselves into all places where humans gather: coffee shops, conferences, libraries, museum, offices, airplanes, and so on.

Collaborative technology, the DIY movement, and co-consumerism set the table for a very important educational revolution that recognizes our peers as the ultimate reality translators, where dialogue is the mother of all didactics and relationships. Dialogue is the ultimate pedagogy. With the proper structure and recognition, peer learning holds a key to enriching, timely, and personalized education for us all.

REFERENCES

Block, P. (2008). *Community: The structure of belonging.* San Francisco: Berrett-Koehler.

Illich, I. (1971). Deschooling society. Retrieved from www.preservenet.com/theory/Illich/Deschooling/intro.html

King, P. (2012). Quora: What would be the memory capacity of our brains if we were to approximate it in terms of bytes? Retrieved from https://www.quora.com/Cognitive-Neuroscience/What-would-be-the-memory-capacity-of-our-brains-if-we-were-to-approximate-it-in-terms-of-bytes

Livingstone, D.W. (2003). *New approaches to life-long learning.* Toronto: Centre for the Study of Education and Work.

Mariuzzo-Raynaud, P. (2012). The first meeting. Retrieved from blog.e-180.com/en/2012/05/portrait-first-meeting/

Mozilla Foundation and Peer 2 Peer University. (2012). Open badges for life-long learning. Retrieved from https://wiki.mozilla.org/File:OpenBadges-Working-Paper_012312.pdf

Topping, K., and Ehly, S. (1998). *Peer-assisted learning.* Mahwah, NJ, & London: Lawrence Erlbaum Associates.

UNESCO. (2005). *Towards knowledge societies.* Paris: UNESCO.

Whitehead, A. (1967). *The aims of education & other essays.* New York: Free Press.

Whitman, N.A. (1988). Peer teaching: To teach isto learn twice. ASHE-ERIC Higher Education Report No. 4.

Willie, C.V. (1994). *Theories of social actions.* New York: General Hall.

Notes

....

....

....

....

....

....

....

....

....

....

....

....

....

....

....

....

notes

RIP OUT AND
FOLD INTO

Notes

notes

Society30: Knowmads and new value creation

RONALD VAN DEN HOFF

'The value creation of tomorrow is born out of the mobility of people, knowledge, and energy.'

'THE OFFICE AS WE KNOW IT IS GONE.'

'WORKING WITH KNOWMADS IS NOT ONLY A NECESSITY, BUT ALSO REWARDING, INSPIRING, AND PURE FUN!'

RONALD VAN DEN HOFF

'WHAT WE REALLY NEED IS AN INNOVUTION!'

'THIS SOCIAL EXCHANGE OF INFORMATION AND KNOWLEDGE LEADS TO COLLABORATION AND EVENTUALLY RESULTS IN "DOING BUSINESS" WITH EACH OTHER IN VALUE NETWORKS.'

SUMMARY

SOCIETY 30: KNOWMADS AND NEW VALUE CREATION
- Ronald van den Hoff -

In a world of limitations imposed by the social market economic model, many countries have found themselves in an economic crisis. The Euro nearly collapsed in 2010, and the threat remains. Large parts of society are under huge pressure. In a power play, banks and other financial institutes are quietly collecting their outlandish profits and bonuses again. It's no wonder that there is polarization in our society. It seems as if it is time for a revolution, or innovation. What we really need is an *innovution*!

Fortunately, a new order is presenting itself. It may still be an undercurrent, but maybe it is the best way to grow. I see more and more people who have clearly chosen how they want to define themselves, their environment, and their relationships with other people. They are the people I call *global citizens*: people of the new world. They want to add meaning to their work and life in a significantly different way, namely by creating value instead of growth. Most of all, the global citizen wants a sustainable society, interconnected through value networks: The *Society30*.

The value creation of tomorrow is born out of the mobility of people, knowledge, and energy. People operate from within their social networks with the same objective of goal sharing. Knowledge is also shared, and results in new value creation. Our co-working formula, Seats2meet.com (S2M), offers venues to facilitate this through co-working, meetings, and collaboration between knowmads and traditional organizations on their way to the Society30. We, as an organization, get back a lot. The return is immense. Our stakeholders appreciate our products and services tremendously, and they help us to position Seats2meet.com on the "free agents" mesh.

In recent years, Western capitalism has done nothing more than shift possessions from the poor to the rich, and it is aided by a complex monetary system that is holding us hostage. This form of modern capitalism does not only grind the faces of the poor, but also our natural resources. Nothing is replenished or compensated, and everything is exploited and bled dry. This is no longer a sustainable model. What we have come to understand as democracy is a poor substitute for the essence of the words "demos" (people) and "krateo" (rule). As a people, we have no say anymore. We have an immense economic problem, but do not expect any solutions from our publishers, car manufacturers, housing contractors or pharmaceutical companies. The established companies are not going to solve this problem and neither will our Western world political- or administrative structures. (van den Hoff, 2011)

The social market economy has ruled in Europe for decades. This system redistributed 65% or more of the national income via the government to all social groups. Traditional capitalism is focused predominately on enriching the stockholders; and, in doing so, it is not only antisocial, but also far from being sustainable. We will not be able to keep the temperature of the planet stable, restore our supply of fossil fuels, and establish international banking control if we hold on to the redistribution policy of the Anglo Saxon (the capitalist macroeconomic model in which levels of regulation and taxes are low, and the government provides relatively fewer services) and/or the Rhineland Economic Model (the capitalist macroeconomic counterpart which is founded on publicly-organized social security). All things considered, this way of redistributing wealth is an outdated concept. Why is our entire economic theory based on the scarcity of people, means and time, resulting in having to make choices? Why do we have to give up one thing if we choose the other? Thinking in terms of limitations, gets us deadlocked in an economic and social sense. We have seen many countries of the European Monetary Union have a larger budget deficit than others. In May 2010, the Euro nearly collapsed because the collaboration and budget discipline was nowhere in sight. This threat still is here. Obviously, this is not desirable in normal times, but in times of crisis, it is deadly. We still reason from the viewpoint of limitations and boundaries, and we are building towering walls around our national interests.

This crisis will persist and will be felt for a long time. Many countries within and outside of Europe will have to put up with a great deal in the next few years. There is nothing but a lot of hot air, which will convert into financial disillusions. Just think of the enormous rise of the aging population in Europe and the fragile situation of the welfare state, the pension system, and the connected level of spending of our municipalities, the rising costs of our health care, and the inevitable depletion of our natural reserves. We are yet to experience the effects of these developments. Hot air, after all, is intangible. And, intangibility translates into financial depreciation.

It seems as if the only system we have is a financial system. It is holding us in The Netherlands hostage as an individual, an organization, and as an EU member state. Actually, our money is simply gone. Already. And, yet, all we can think of is to produce more money, inject it into the existing structures, curtail expenditures with that money (!), and impose the largest part of that burden on the part of society that can't carry it. Entire industries are still crying out for more money to bear the costs for new business models that are meant to postpone their end of life cycle yet again. These long-established companies are apparently not able to self-innovate and unfortunately terminating the business is not part of their corporate strategy. At the same time, they are blocking opportunities for newcomers with their unwieldiness, their managerial jumble, and their monopolization of the big funds.

Large parts of society are under huge pressure. In their power play, banks and other financial institutes are quietly collecting their outlandish profits and bonuses again. It's no wonder that there is polarization in our society. It seems as if it is time for a revolution, or innovation. What we really need is an *innovution*!

KNOWMADS IN THE WORLD OF SOCIETY30
>>

Fortunately, there is moss growing on the rocks, the convolvulus is creeping through the cracks, and the desert plants only need a few raindrops to bloom. A new order is presenting itself. It may still be an undercurrent, but maybe it is the best way to grow. A moorland fire if you will. I see more and more people who have clearly chosen how they want to define themselves, their environments, and their relationships with other people.

They are the people I call *global citizens*: people of the new world. These Society30 citizens cannot and will not deal with the thinking of the establishment anymore. They want to add meaning to their work and life in a significantly different way, namely by creating value instead of growth. Most of all, the global citizen wants a sustainable society. *The Society30*.

I think these global citizens – who are increasing in number daily – are the pillars, which support Society30, the society that really operates better!

Global citizens, people of the world:

- Are open, transparent, and unbiased in taking the "traditional answers" for granted;
- See differences between people and cultures as a source of creativity;
- Want to learn with and from each other, grow and work together;
- Are interested in other cultures and introspective of their own culture;
- See themselves as part of the world and not specifically as citizens of a nation or city; and,
- Act from transnational values and standards.

Hundreds of millions of people in the world move around without restraints, literally unbounded, across borders all over the planet. Sometimes they do this physically, but more often they do so digitally through the Internet: the World Wide Web. These people of the world are no longer bound to old organizations. They have organized themselves in virtual social networks. They have started to create value in a different way. They do not work according to a formal organizational structure. They guide themselves. They are themselves. Their social connections show great creative vitality and unleash an enormous amount of energy. From within their self-awareness they respect the individuality of anybody. People of the world are not after personal enrichment at the expense of others. They share, and they are prepared to do a lot for someone else, without expecting a monetary reward. I think it is both exciting and fun to be such a person, a knowmad of the world of Society30.

In his book, *The Cubrix*, van Marrewijk (2011) argues that we are ready for a new economic model – and, with that, a new social and political model for the new Society30. This economic model is called the Interdependent Economy, a social economic value system based on *solidarity, sustainability*, and *reciprocity*. Actually, it is a logical next step in the development of our society. History shows us a certain evolutionary order of ranking in different economic systems that had a limited shelf life. Every system was suitable for the specific circumstances of that period. Economic systems are transient, which is caused by changing environmental factors. So, at a certain point in time, these economic systems no longer connect to reality.

The real power within the Interdependent Economy of the Society30 will shift to the consumer or the citizen. As it happens, these people organize themselves. They want to participate. They want to engage with suppliers. These engaged consumers or "prosumers" (see esp. Toffler, 1980; Tapscott, 1995) want to co-create in order to develop customized products and services of impeccable quality. Transparency, accountability, and authenticity are the core values. The Internet makes these affairs transparent, making the prosumer more educated than ever about what's for sale at which price or on how your organization interprets its social role and responsibility. The prosumer has a whole range of alternative suppliers, provided by his or her social network, at its disposal. The prosumer wants to choose, can choose, and will choose. Hence, the Organization30 will have to seek an alliance with prosumers to ensure that consumers are participating at an early stage, and, in doing so, determine what is being produced and how. Call this *social business*, if you like. In this case, it is not about the product itself. More and more products are being packaged as a service. Many people want to have access to something, but do not necessarily have to own it. In their book, *What's mine is yours*, the authors Botsman and Rodgers (2010) call this development *collaborative consumption*. I prefer to call it *collaborative prosumption*.

NETWORK VALUE CREATION
>>

Collaborative prosumption means when we create economic value in the Interdependent Economy, we are moving automatically away from the traditional value chain toward value networks (Allee, 2008; Benkler, 2006).

There is no particular fixed connection between network members in a value network; the network is not always visible as a group. Generally, a value network has a few core members – including a potential client – complemented with "occasional-collaborators" and some other people who contribute incidentally and/or if required (resonance). The core workers often do not know the marginal participants, while the source of knowledge is not always visible either; it is more of a cloud. Or as John Moravec is known to call it figuratively in his lectures, "a plate of spaghetti and meatballs."

Value networks like this – I like to call these *Social Economic Entities* – almost exhibit Al Qaida-like structures and movements (van den Hoff, 2011). Teamwork is a great concept, but working in a value network goes beyond the old team philosophy. It already starts with a different understanding of objectives. In traditional team-based organizations, the targeted goals are usually clearly defined, as is the road that reaches it, such as the allocation of tasks and responsibility. A value network is mainly characterized by shared points of view and a path of creation that is mutually discovered in a context of collective responsibility. In the collaboration with or within organizations, the community leader facilitates the process as much as possible, but you cannot call this managing. There is an open structure: for new knowledge and contacts, one can make an appeal to the entire outside world. The same goes for the capturing and making of the acquired knowledge by the value network available. The old "team thinking" is disposed to keeping this within their walls, but value creation is, of course, best served by open connections.

For "customers" it is therefore not always clear who bears the final responsibility for value creation, while it is not always clear to the network members how revenues will be shared or how copyright issues are dealt with. We actually need a new legal form for these kinds of occasional networks or constellations. I propose occasional formations that are each legally organized as a Social Economic Entity. Within these entities, arrangements can provide insight for all stakeholders, including the final client. Whereas regular organizational teams or departments tend to mark their territories and build ivory towers, value networks have the ability to connect to each other. Individual members of value networks can organize themselves from one spot. In part, this increases the data portability between networks on a daily basis. This is how boundaries continue to dissolve: Value networks are extraordinarily dynamic and flow into each other. That is why it is so difficult for outsiders to understand: It is not always an obviously recognizable team or project group that is on the job. The work is also no longer done between four walls under a single roof, with the name of the organization on the façade of the building. The places where new value creation takes place are hard to identify... they can be found in what I like to call *The Mesh*, THE network of networks. Mesh networks can be described as a network system of nodes where each node must not only capture and disseminate its own data, but also serve as a *relay* for other nodes. That is, nodes must collaborate to propagate the data in the network ("Mesh networking," n.d.).

Society30 organizations are innovative network organizations within their own Mesh. They will grow towards so-called real time companies: network organizations with permanently connected stakeholders, where informal and formal relationships flourish. The Internet and other (mobile) technologies are optimally used to create value and are continuously working on facilitating the collaboration process. The network stakeholders are convinced of the fact that thinking in terms of relevancy and reliability can maximize interconnectivity. Organizations that are able to put this into practice can look forward to a successful right to exist, whereby working innovatively and creatively with ,and in the interests of stakeholders, a meaningful product or service of actual value is created. This is what I like to call *Organization30*: a sustainable organizational ecosystem where people can be proud of the stakeholder value that is created. Obviously this Organization30 has a "somewhat different design" than we have been used to. And ,in building it, there is a big role for our knowmads.

Stakeholders of the Organization30 want to be increasingly involved with the realization of services or products. This contributes to that "special" user experience. Every experience from incidental co-creation to a full collaboration enhances the feeling that it is all about you, and, as an additional advantage, delivering a much more superior product or service. So much better, in fact, that the eventual sticker price, whether that be monetary or social capital, has become secondary as a selection criteria for doing business, procurement, and collaboration. In order to give the stakeholders that feeling of authenticity, and in order to co-create with them, the organization has to connect with them and start a dialogue. To gain access to a whole network of stakeholders, the modern decisive organization can do itself a favor by developing a solid social media strategy. The starting point is that all communication moments (so called touch points) are linked directly between a stakeholder and the person within the Organization30 who is directly responsible for that part of the service or product. This requires dynamic and flexible internal processes and a large extent of operational freedom for the people involved. Some innovative companies let stakeholders interact among themselves even without any "employee" involvement in the official form of a webcare team, a helpdesk (like the UK-based Telco Giffgaff), service department, or sales desk (like the Dutch based co-working locations operator Seats2meet.com).

Through the network of inter-human contact, a permanent connectivity comes into being between the organization, its people, and its other stakeholders. This social exchange of information and knowledge leads to collaboration and eventually results in "doing business" with each other in value networks.

So, the most important value creation players in the Interdependent Economy, who are no longer large organizations, but increasingly small to medium sized networked enterprises, are complemented by an army of independent professionals – knowmads (Moravec, 2008). We're talking about a new generation of people who consider virtual social communication to be normal and find sharing generative for the common good; and, they find the use of the Internet common practice. The collapse or even the disappearance of large traditional organizational entities will accelerate this process.

The number of knowmads is growing fast. In 2002, in the United States alone, there were already over 33 million *free agents*, another term for knowmads, about one in four American workers (Pink, 2002).

In The Netherlands, we see the same picture: over one million traditional employees will retire in the coming 5 years, a process that started in 2010. They will be replaced by a staggering number of knowmads. In 2020, we estimate this Dutch group to be larger than 2.5 million people, representing 40% (!) of the total workforce.

The Organization30 is *forced* to collaborate with knowmads in the process of survival by new value creation since there are not enough regular employees left.

NEW VALUE CREATION: THE 3RD SPACE
>>

If you want to claim your position in the clusters of new value networks as an organization *en route* to tomorrow in The Mesh, you will have to work with minimal standardization and a new

Co-workers, knowmads, free agents, self-enterprising professionals...

During a recent meeting with the Seats2meet.com team, I asked one of our "employees" Lukie, "can you fetch the flip-chart, I want to draw something." Lukie is very smart. This is how she describes herself on her social media profile: "I got my bachelor in Liberal Arts & Sciences and majored in New Media. During my studies at the University of Utrecht, I researched new media, games and digital culture. I also invented and implemented an open-source, cross-media concept." Yet, after my request she looked at me quizzically and with a bit uncertainly. I asked her, "do you know what a flip-chart is?" "No," she replied timidly.

Voilá: the "knowmad-employees." They know everything about cross-media, social media, apps, co-creation, prosumption, crowd sourcing, and user generated content. And, they know about augmented reality, embedding, MOOCs, and MMORPGs as well. They have a significant Internet presence. They do not automatically think of money when they talk about value. Transparency and sharing knowledge are second nature to them. Knowmads are looking for a learning and work environment that connects to the way of communicating they have been cultivating privately for years. And, one that stimulates them to learn and develop themselves during their whole lifetime.

But they do not know what a flip chart is.

informal corporate culture based on trust and open communication. Only then can you seriously make an appeal to autonomy and entrepreneurship in order to excel internally as well as externally around a dynamic organization. It is not a matter of "being social on the side." It requires a complete new vision on organizing. A vision to rethink the order of things. A vision that answers the question of how to challenge someone within the new value networks to feel, think, and operate with his entire capacity for the value of co-creation; and, how to supply the stakeholders of relevant information at the right time, so that they can operate independently and thus perform. And, a vision for a style of leadership to keep all of this on the right track.

The value creation of tomorrow is born out of the mobility of people, knowledge, and energy. People operate from within their social networks with the same objective, sharing goals. Knowledge is also being shared, resulting in new knowledge and thus creating new value. In Society30, we are going to collaborate in a different way. And, we do that within open and flat organizations: Social network organizations that are in harmony with their environment, and are therefore sustainable. Individuals

profile and organize themselves on the web and connect with peers on platforms like Facebook and LinkedIn. Their communication tools are called blogs, wikis, Tweets, Skype, or Google+. For their physical meet-ups, they use event software. Obviously, they communicate in various languages, but the Web translates for them. Groups of people can collaborate, grow organically, and fuse. Computers and software become a service. Many services are free, and content and data are abundant. Thus, access becomes more important than possession, and that becomes a leading driver for Society30. The virtual social networks are the glue for this new value creation.

Sustainable value creation needs the connection between the old financial business models and the new social business models. When the Organization30 collaborates with knowmads, the value creation process is organized through the Social Economic Entities. That means that the known social network groups like Facebook and LinkedIn are a mere starting point for this value creation. Only when traditional organizations start to realize this, they can start thinking in terms of value networks instead of traditional value chains.

These new value networks need virtual and physical locations to meet and to collaborate. The office as we know it is gone. The traditional school, library, and meeting center will follow.

We need new physical locations in new geographical locations where people can meet, work, exchange information, and more. It is a revival of the 3rd Place (Oldenburg, 1999). Regus, the largest provider of flexible workspaces in the world, labels 3rd Places in their 2011 annual statement as, "exciting opportunities to grow the business" (Regus, 2012).

We have taken this development even a step further. Our co-working formula, Seats2meet.com (S2M), offers venues for co-working, meetings, and collaboration between knowmads and traditional organizations on their way to the Society30. It is a super hub and spoke network of physical co-work, office, and meeting locations, where besides dedicated locations, even individual co-working places in 3rd party office buildings (belonging to companies who believe it is an asset to welcome outsiders within their walls) participate.

Our meeting rooms and office spaces are booked by regular clients and knowmads who pay a fee per seat used (and not per room). Pricing is based on a sophisticated yield management system.

For knowmads who just want a place to work, meet, and connect with others, we offer coworking spaces, WiFi, beverages, and even an occasional lunch *free of charge* in old monetary terms. "Free" means however "no free lunch": upon reservation, the bookers/ co-workers tell the system, and all members of the S2M network, what topics he/she is working on, where his/her interests are, and more. This way, the booker commits him/herself to the network: he/she is available for unexpected meetings and maybe called upon by traditional clients in the meeting rooms to share their expertise and knowledge. Payment by knowmads is therefore done by means of social capital. As traditional organizations in transition are renting regular meeting rooms in traditional Euros, we have created a parallel monetary system linking traditional *and* social capital.

On top of every physical Seats2meet. com location, there is a real-time virtual blanket of information and knowledge of people present that can be cleverly used. In this way, co-working and meeting other people at Seats2meet.com locations become unexpectedly relevant, useful, and become a new way to connect and form new ways for cooperation – serendipitously.

We go even further: we provide, free of charge for every stakeholder, a dynamic (mobile) software platform where professionals can interact, virtually work, and meet. Also, when a physical meeting room is booked through the S2M online booking system, a virtual meeting space is generated automatically and linked to the group of people attending that meeting, training session, or conference. This service is offered in close cooperation with the Helsinki-based company, Meetin.gs. These virtual meeting rooms or classrooms are used to interconnect participants upfront, to communicate with participants before and after the physical session, and to communicate organizational details around that meeting.

With these software systems, we enable our stakeholders to collaborate real-time within the Social Economic Entities of the world of Society30. In blurring these virtual and the physical products, services, and logistic com-

ponents around our physical locations, we have created an organization in what Pine & Korn (2011) name in their latest book *Infinite possibility*, the *3rd Space*: "The digital frontier, lying at the intersection of digital technology and offering innovation, beckons companies seeking to create new customer value by mining its rich veins of possibility... But by far the greatest value will come from those innovations that create third spaces that fuse the real and the virtual."

Thus, the 3rd Place has become the 3rd Space. This 3rd Space enables us at Seats2meet.com to offer an unique, tailor-made experience, with a serendipitous educational element, to all our stakeholders. "Experiences" at Seats2meet.com locations become "transformations," in line with Pine & Gilmore's (2011) theory of the "Progression of Economic Value," where "transformations" are the subsequent drivers of value creation after traditional "experiences."

We, as an organization, get back a lot. The return is immense. Our stakeholders appreciate our products and services tremendously, and they help us to position Seats2meet.com on the "free agents" mesh. They create an enormous flow of buzz on the Web (we used to call that PR in the old days); they feed us with tips, reviews, knowledge, and their time (that used to be called "marketing"); and, they actively promote us to other knowmads and to corporate and governmental organizations (that used to be called "sales"). Whenever they have "real business," they book their training and meeting rooms at Seats2meet.com locations without asking for a discount because the system provides them with tremendous value. Therefore, at Seats2meet.com we no longer have a PR, sales, or marketing, or reservation department. How do you think that works out for our operational costs? The still growing army of "fans" who do our commercial activities is staggering.

With (potential) co-working operators worldwide, we now share our co-working reservation and yield management system, the property management software, and our operational knowledge (partly free) through a special program called Myownseats2meet.com. In The Netherlands alone, we have grown our business within two years from one location to over 50 locations, while, internationally, we are on the brink of making the same waves.

So, being a pioneer in the World of Society30, I certainly can attest to the fact that as an Organization30 working with knowmads is not only a necessity, but also rewarding, inspiring, and pure fun!

REFERENCES

Allee, V. (2008). Value network analysis and value conversion of tangible assets. *Journal of Intellectual Capital, 9* (1), 5-24.

Benkler, Y. (2006). The wealth of networks: How social production transforms markets and freedom. Yale: Yale University Press.

Botsman, R., & Rogers, R. (2010). *What's mine is yours: The rise of collaborative consumption.* New York: HarperCollins.

van den Hoff, R. (2011). *Society 3.0.* Utrecht: Stichting Society 3.0.

van Marrewijk, M. (2011). *De Cubrix: Zicht op organisatieontwikkeling en performanceverbetering.* Ronde Tafel, SU De.

Mesh networking. (n.d.). In Wikipedia. Retrieved August 3, 2012, from en.wikipedia.org/wiki/Mesh_networking

Moravec, J. (2008). Towards Society 3.0: A new paradigm for 21st century education. Keynote lecture presented at *ASOMEX Technology Conference: Education for children of the 21st Century.* Monterrey, Mexico.

Oldenburg, R. (1999). *The great good place: Cafes, coffee shops, bookstores, bars, hair salons, and other hangouts at the heart of the community* (Vol. 3). Washington DC: Marlowe & Company.

Pine, J. B., & Gilmore, J. H. (2011). *The experience economy, updated edition.* Boston: Harvard Business Review Press.

Pine, J. B., & Korn, K. C. (2011). *Infinite possibility.* San Francisco: Berret-Koehler Publishers.

Pink, H. D. (2002). *Free agent nation: The future of working for yourself* (Vol. 1). New York: Business Plus.

Regus. (2012, March 20). Regus 2011 full year presentation. Retrieved August 3, 2012, from www.regus.com/images/2011-Full-year-presentation_tcm8-49854.pdf

Tapscott, D. (1995). *Promise and peril in the age of the networked intelligence.* New York: Mc-Graw-Hill.

Toffler, A. (1980). *The third wave.* New York: Bantam Books.

Notes

FILL THESE PAGES WITH

notes

EVERYTHING THAT COMES
TO MIND

Notes

notes

Notes

Afterword

As economically and socially profound as the implications of the Knowmad Society are, as described in this book, the political implications are even greater. It would be a mistake of profound proportions to assume all Americans, or for that matter all Chinese, have access to the Knowmad Society.

Those with "Knowmad" skills are set apart from those without those skills. To prevent a further widening and deepening chasm between knowledge "haves" and "have-nots," democratic societies and governments must dramatically increase opportunities for the information and communications unskilled to enter the Knowmad Society. This will be especially true for poor, urban youth who are much less inclined to have computer learning opportunities and the skills they produce.

The early 19th century transition from an agrarian to an industrial society took decades. Young people from rural and small town America found it necessary to migrate en masse to urban America to seek job opportunities in the emerging mechanized and industrialized society. Mid-career craftsmen, the so-called "buggy-whip" makers, also found it necessary to learn new skills on the steel and auto assembly lines. Many failed to do so and simply became victims of the transition. The emerging industrial economy transformed the face and structure of American society and its economy. And it transformed American politics as well. After much civil strife and against considerable resistance, labor unions emerged to represent the financial and safety concerns of industrial workers. Those same unions came to play a dominant role in the fortunes of the Democratic Party in the age of Roosevelt.

As the assembly line came to characterize the industrial age, so the computer and its myriad wireless spin-offs have come to characterize the post-industrial communications and information age. The former aggregated skilled and semi-skilled workers. The latter are creating virtual networks among those who possess the magic technologies and the skills to manipulate them. Since those networks transcend national boundaries, however, they are also integrating transnationally. Today, lawyers in Denver, Colorado, have as much, or more in common, with lawyers in London, Tokyo, and Beijing than they do with non-knowmads in their own communities. The same would be true of educators, businesspeople, government officials, and many others.

The implications for traditional political structures is enormous. Politics and public policies emerge from shared interests and loyalties. As transnational knowmad networks become more intricate, shared concerns will begin to impact domestic and international public policies. International knowmad networks will begin to insist on common economic policies in trade, finance, taxation, resource allocation, travel, information access, and a host of other concerns. What is good for my network in Rome, Dubai, Shanghai, Moscow, and Copenhagen is good for me.

The nagging question remains: what to do with those who have not entered or do not have access to the Knowmad Universe? As too much of a generation was lost economically and socially in the transition from agrarian to industrial society, so the same massive dislocation cannot be permitted to occur during our current transition from industrial to the knowmad information and communications age of the 21st century.

Great care must be taken not to create further stratified societies in the developed, developing, and under-developed world. The United States witnessed serious urban unrest in the 1960s and 1970s. London and other cities have experienced the same in more recent times. And the "Arab Spring" of early 2011 in North Africa and the Middle East arose, in part, by widening divisions between haves and have-nots and between elites and unemployed youth. Political instability springs from despair at seeing others nearby who have greater access to opportunity by virtue of class or privilege.

Politically, it behooves Knowmad Society to extend its reach as broadly as possible. Those inside the Society must demand public policies that open its doors and its windows. What could be better for a ghetto high-schooler than to have a inexpensive computer and a semester in a nearby foreign culture. This is a mandate both for governments and for capitalist enterprises as well, especially those which seek stable societies well into the 21st century.

A broad-based Knowmad Society will require public policies of training in technology and computer skills, revamping a good deal of traditional public education, a new influx of teachers competent in the knowledge and communications skills, rigorous insistence on student performance by both schools and families, increased insistence on core competencies in science and math, and a nation dedicated to a high level of international competitiveness. In all these categories, the United States has much ground to travel.

But the political implications of the Knowmad Society extend to the arena of national and international security as well. The Westphalian age of the nation-state, post-1647, based security concerns on the bargain between the state and the nation: the state (government) would protect the nation (the people) in exchange for their loyalty to the state. Thereafter, wars were conducted by uniformed national armies meeting in more or less orderly combat in the field of battle. That bargain collapsed on September 11, 2001, when the mightiest state in world history failed to protect its citizens from a new kind of conflict.

The 21st century features a host of new realities, including failed and failing states, climate degradation, viral pandemics, mass south-north migrations, proliferation of weapons of mass destruction, terrorism, the rise of ethnic nationalism, fundamentalism, tribalism, and a host of phenomena more characteristic of the 11th than the 20th century. These and other new realities have two things in common: they cannot be solved by traditional military means; and they cannot be addressed by one nation, including the United States, alone.

The rise of the Knowmad Society coincides with a revolutionary new century. Globalization and information have eroded the sovereignty of the nation-state and that in turn has helped transform the nature of warfare into an era of irregular, unconventional conflict. The Knowmad Society's citizens, then, must be strongly encouraged to help fashion a new concept of security for this new age, one that breaks down, rather than erects, new walls.

That security concept and the strategies it produces will necessarily be more internationalist, more multi-dimensional (not just military), and more collaborative. The public health service of advanced and other nations must be networked to quarantine pandemics before they escape confinement. The International Atomic Energy Agency must be given greater intrusive inspection authority to detect production of weapons of mass destruction. Advanced nations must manage the transition of failing states to

prevent emergence of ancient tribal and ethnic hostilities. A serious international climate stabilization regime must be created rapidly.

Thus, it is incumbent on all those who participate in the Knowmad Society to take seriously the duty they share to use their skills and competencies to address these new security concerns.

The key to international security in the emerging international Knowmad Society will be in anticipation of, rather than reaction to, crises, in multi-national collaborative networking and cooperation, and in threat reduction through preventive measures.

If the Knowmad Society creates new international elite networks, if it widens the gap between those in the "know" and those not, and if it fails to understand the post-Westphalian transformation of the nation-state, it will not have advanced the human condition to say the least.

If, however, those with the good fortune to enter the inner sanctum of this new society strive to be inclusive and to broaden its membership as much as possible, if they throw open the doors and windows of knowledge and access to as many young people, including especially the disadvantaged, as possible, and if they use the networks of knowledge upon which the society is based to break down ancient barriers of tribe, clan, and the elite, then the promise of this new century can truly be realized.

The emerging Knowmad Society has profound opportunities and even more profound public responsibilities.

GARY HART
KITTREDGE, COLORADO

Notes

notes

Author biographies

and collaborations in the United States, Latin America, and Europe. In addition to editing Knowmad Society, he is the co-author of the book *Invisible learning* (2011, University of Barcelona Press).
Twitter: @moravec

JOHN W. MORAVEC is an education futurist, co-initiator of the Invisible Learning project, and the editor of Education Futures (ISSN 1940-0934, www.educationfutures.com). John's research and action scholarship agenda are focused on exploring the convergence of globalization, innovation society, and accelerating change in human knowledge development; and, building positive futures for knowledge creation systems which are approaching an increasingly complex and ambiguous future. His work focuses on exploring the emerging "Knowmad Paradigm," and the new approaches to leadership and human capital development required. His work is global, and he is most actively engaged in research

THIEU BESSELINK is founder of The Learning Lab, a think-tank for social change. He is a learning innovator, researcher, philosopher, and social entrepreneur. He teaches social entrepreneurship, action research, system innovation, and leadership learning at Amsterdam University and Utrecht University. He wrote his multidisciplinary doctoral thesis with Profs. Richard Sennett and Neil Walker at the European University Institute and LSE on authority and leadership in an open society. He also studied at the theater academy in Florence; arts at Utrecht University College; law, organization, culture and management at Utrecht University; political philosophy at Bologna University; and completed an MSc in philosophy and urban studies at London School of Economics.

Thieu was a political and strategic adviser to the mayor and vice mayors of the City of Dordrecht; adviser to British ministers Bill Rammell and Gordon Brown for the Fabian Society; an executive coach; a board member of the Utrecht University Department of Law; an executive board member of the Dutch Student Union; an editorial board member of Scienceguide; and, a worked at NPI - Dutch institute for organizational development and leadership. Currently, he serves as a member of the audit committee of the Sirius innovation fund for the stimulation of excellence in Dutch higher education.

Twitter: @besselink

EDWIN DE BREE is an organizational survival guide, and helps companies survive the post-hierarchic network society. He is a co-founder of the hybrid project, Entrepreneurial Organizations, in collaboration with Bianca Stokman and the Leadership & Entrepreneurship Centre De Baak. He is also co-founder of the De Koers Sudbury-type school in The Netherlands. The school is built on a democratic platform where young people prepare themselves for the knowmadic world.

Edwin is committed to the reframing of schools and organizations toward supporting the development and utilization of human potential. He regularly conducts masterclasses, facilitates workshops, and leads projects for client companies. He is also a co-founder of Groei-Coöperatie, and has the most fun when he builds employee-owned-and-managed companies.

Twitter: @edwin3punt0

CRISTÓBAL COBO is a researcher at the Oxford Internet Institute at the University of Oxford. He coordinates research on innovation, open educational practices and the future of the Internet (EU-FP7). He is an award recipient from the British Council of Economic and Social Research (ESRC), and he earned a PhD cum laudem in Communication Sciences at Universitat Autònoma de Barcelona, Spain. He is the co-author of *Invisible learning* (2011, University of Barcelona Press), and speaks frequently in Europe and the Americas. His blog at the Oxford Internet Institute is online at blogs.oii. ox.ac.uk/cobo – and his blog, e-rgonomic (in Spanish), is online at ergonomic.wordpress. com.

Twitter: @cristobalcobo

GARY HART has been extensively involved in international law and business, as a strategic advisor to major U.S. corporations, and as a teacher, author and lecturer. Gary Hart represented the State of Colorado in the United States Senate from 1975 to 1987. In 1984 and 1988, he was a candidate for his party's nomination for President. He is currently Scholar in Residence at the University of Colorado and Distinguished Fellow at the Center for Strategic and International Studies. He is chair of the Threat Reduction Advisory Council at the Department of Defense, was vice-chair of the Secretary of Homeland Security's Advisory Council, former chair of the Council for a Livable World, chair of the American Security Project, and co-chair of the US-Russia Commission.
Gary Hart was co chair of the U.S. Commission on National Security for the 21st Century.

The Commission performed the most comprehensive review of national security since 1947, predicted the terrorist attacks on America, and proposed a sweeping overhaul of U.S. national security structures and policies for the post- Cold War new century and the age of terrorism. For 15 years, Senator Hart was Senior Counsel to Coudert Brothers, a multinational law firm with offices in thirty-two cities located in nineteen countries around the world. He has traveled extensively to the former Soviet Union, Europe, the Far East and Latin America. Senator Hart resides with his family in Kittredge, Colorado.

CHRISTEL HARTKAMP-BAKKER is co-founder of De Kampanje, a Sudbury-type school in Amersfoort, The Netherlands. Christel, together with her husband, Peter, have been involved in democratic education since 2002, when the first democratic schools developed in The Netherlands. She has been actively involved in the European Democratic Education Community as a council-member, and developed her expertise on the wide variety of approaches that exist between democratic schools.
Christel received a PhD degree in production geology, and built a previous career in the oil industry. She now primarily focuses her work on the establishment of strong Sudbury schools, and works as a staff member at De Kampanje. She is author of the book: *De Kampanje - Sudbury Valley school in Nederland* (2009).
Twitter: @chartkamp

RONALD VAN DEN HOFF is co-owner of CDEF Holding BV, and maintains a portfolio of companies active on the borderline of the hospitality industry and the world of social media. CDEF operates innovative, disruptive, Blue Ocean formulas such as the co-working and meeting centers Seats 2meet.com, the virtual eco-systeem Mindz.com, the internet communication company Cyberdigma BV, and the Meeting Plaza convention centers. Ronald holds a degree in hotel management, and, after holding various senior management positions in the hospitality and tourism industry, he has been an entrepreneur since 1985. He is also an Internet/social media strategist, and advises many international companies and governmental organizations on topics such as e-commerce, innovation, and economic trends. He is author of the book, *Society30* (2011). Twitter: @rvandenhoff

CHRISTINE RENAUD is a Montreal-based social entrepreneur who is passionate about self-directed learning and community-based learning. As the CEO of E-180, she is responsible for managing the educational direction, sales, funding, partnerships, and the community building behind E-180.

Prior to E-180, Christine completed her MEd work as a Frank Knox Fellow at the Harvard Graduate School of Education, focusing on informal learning and alternative educational approaches. In 2008, she worked as a podcast producer for Learning Matters in New York. She consults as a social media expert for various social projects & founded #ClavEd, a weekly Twitter meet-up for French-speaking educators. She was recognized in 2006 by L'Actualité as the most promising young leader in education in Québec. More recently, the Montreal's Mayor Foundation elected her as a fellow for her work with E-180. She is often invited to share her experience on peer learning in public events, including as #140edu in New York, SXSW Interactive, and Ignite in Montreal. Twitter: @christinerenaud

PIETER SPINDER was born in Friesland, The Netherlands, into an entrepreneurial family. Despite being expelled from secondary school, he ultimately earned a bachelors degree in marketing. He then started several different companies, including Office Dump (second-hand photocopier sales) and The Marketing Factory, a marketing consultancy.

Pieter has been a lecturer at the University of Applied Science in Amsterdam since 1998 where he teaches in the areas of e-commerce, creativity management, innovation, sustainable leadership and entrepreneurship, and the Knowmadic Learning Lab minor.

He is a co-founder of the KaosPilots Netherlands business school in Rotterdam; and, in 2009, he co-founded the Knowmads Business School in Amsterdam.
Twitter: @pieterspinder

BIANCA STOKMAN has a background in organizational psychology, human resource sciences, and also studied voice at the Conservatory of Utrecht. She started her career as an HR officer for tradition-ally-structured organizations, where only one expertise was required for job performance. She then joined De Baak Management Center for nine years, which is a renowned Dutch training institute. Founded upon the Humanist Tradition, the institute's focus is on the individual, the individual's effective interaction within the organization or company — and, within society. There, she experienced what it means to have all of your talents appre-ciated and challenged in an organization. This environment enabled her to making her own choices, set her own bound-aries, and direct her personal growth. In 2011, she started her own business, Messing & Groef, as a trainer and coach for personal and leadership development. She is fascinated by the biological foundations of human behavior and learning.
Twitter: @messingengroef

MARTINE EYZENGA is a graphic artist and information designer. Her creative work is featured in the core designs of the PICNIC Festival, Project Dreamschool, and Operation Education social innovation platforms. "Design is not about spicing up an item. It is about analyzing the question, solving a problem, and making it fun."
www.diezijnvaardig.nl

SYMEN VEENSTRA (Enkeling) is an Amsterdam-based visual artist with roots in graffiti and graphic design. His work is focused on illustration, typography, and portraiture. Sometimes he likes to mix all three together.
Twitter: @enkeling

Glossary

Terms and key ideas used in Knowmad Society

ACCELERATING CHANGE/ACCELERATING RETURNS: Kurzweil (1999) postulates a Law of Accelerating Returns: "as order exponentially increases, time exponentially speeds up (that is, the time interval between salient events grows shorter as time passes)" (p. 30). Technological advances (e.g., achievements in the development of agriculture, industrialization) are represented by s-curves. As time progresses, the rate of technical advancement increases, and multiple significant advancements will occur concurrently. If combined and plotted as a line, the multiple s-curves stack to form a "J-curve" shape that approximates an exponential rate of technological change over time. The Law of Accelerating Returns is modeled after Moore's Law (1965) of technological development of integrated circuits.

CO-CONSTRUCTIVISM: The leverage of relational horizontality where all participants in a learning system engage in teaching and learning. This allows for the "general reconceptualization of knowledge in any social formation..." (Hakken, 2003, p. p. 306).

INNOVATION: Innovation is the beneficial application of creativity to solve a new problem or provide a new solution to an existing challenge.

INNOVATION ECONOMY/ INNOVATION SOCIETY: Activities in the innovation society are centered on the innovative applications of knowledge as opposed to agricultural, industrial or information-based inputs.

INNOVUTION: Disruptive innovations.

INTERDISCIPLINARITY: Research or action that connects two or more discipline areas together.

KNOWLEDGE: An internalized combination of tacit and explicit personal understandings of data and information that can be exhibited as expertise or skills.

KNOWLEDGE ECONOMY/KNOWLEDGE SOCIETY: The knowledge economy was first defined by Drucker (1969) to describe the emerging impact that information technology advances would have on the economy and on society. Drucker (1993) describes the social impact of the knowledge economy on individuals in the knowledge society:

> In the knowledge society into which we are moving, individuals are central. Knowledge is not impersonal, like money. Knowledge does not reside in a book, a databank, a software program; they contain only information. Knowledge is always embodied in a person, carried by a person; created, augmented, or improved by a person; applied by a person; taught by a person, and passed on by a person. The shift to the knowledge society therefore puts the person in the center. (p. 210)

KNOWMAD SOCIETY: An emerging proto-paradigm driven by 1) accelerating technological and social change; 2) continuing globalization and the horizontalization of knowledge and relationships; and, 3) an innovation-oriented society fueled by knowmads.

KNOWMADS: Nomadic knowledge and innovation workers who are creative, imaginative, and innovative, and able to work with almost anybody, anytime, and anywhere. Their individual, personal knowledge gives them a competitive advantage over other workers.

LEAPFROG: To jump over obstacles to achieve goals. It means to get ahead of the competition or the present state of the art through innovative, time-and-cost-saving means. Leapfrogging denotes leadership created by looking ahead and acting "over the horizon" of contemporary possibilities.

MINDWARE: Technologies that support our imaginations, creativity, and capacities to innovate.

SOCIETY 1.0: The agricultural to industrial-based society that was largely present through the 18th century through the end of the 20th century.

SOCIETY 2.0: Knowledge-based society that values the creation of personally-constructed meanings that defy the absolute objectivity of Society 1.0's industrial information model.

SOCIETY 3.0 (MORAVEC VARIATION): (see Knowmad Society)

SOCIETY30 (VAN DEN HOFF VARIATION): The new era to come that is smart, simple and sustainable.

TECHNOLOGICAL SINGULARITY: "At this point, socioeconomic and technological change will occur so rapidly that, to an outside observer, it would be impossible to discern what changes will take place or how. Human imagination can provide visions of what the Singularity's event horizon could be like, but, due to the exponential rate of change, what lies beyond is not predictable. In other words, the Technical Singularity marks the limit of human imagination." (Moravec, 2007).

TECHNOLOGY: Tools, knowledge and skills that may be applied to augment the capabilities of humans and human systems.

THIRD SPACE: A place that fuses the real and the virtual. Introduced in Pine & Korn (2011).

TRANSDISCIPLINARITY: Research or action that blends different discipline areas together, creating a new, third discipline.

REFERENCES

Drucker, P. F. (1969). *The age of discontinuity: Guidelines to our changing society.* New York: Harper & Row.

Drucker, P. F. (1985). *Innovation and entrepreneurship: Practice and principles* (1st ed.). New York: Harper & Row.

Hakken, D. (2003). *The knowledge landscapes of cyberspace.* New York: Routledge.

Kurzweil, R. (1999). *The age of spiritual machines: When computers exceed human intelligence.* New York: Viking.

Moore, G. E. (1965). Cramming more components onto integrated circuits. *Electronics Magazine, 38*(8).

Moravec, J. W. (2007). A New Paradigm of knowledge production in Minnesota higher education: A Delphi study. Thesis (Ph D), University of Minnesota, 2008. Major: Educational policy and administration. Retrieved from www.lib.umn.edu/articles/proquest.phtml

Pine, J. B., & Korn, K. C. (2011). *Infinite possibility.* San Francisco: Berret-Koehler Publishers.

Appendix
Workshops offered at the Knowmads Business School

This appendix provides examples of the workshops at the Knowmads Business School in Amsterdam. We divided them in six categories: Entrepreneurship and new business, personal leadership, body movement, social innovation and sustainability, project and process design, and marketing and creativity.

ENTREPRENEURSHIP AND NEW BUSINESS
Turning your (business) dream into reality

- Social responsibility & NGOs – Selma Steenhuisen
  What are the roles of NGOs in our society and how do they work?
- Power lab / Satori Game - Huib Kraaijeveld
  Role-playing simulation on how we (automatically) behave in hierarchies.
- New business concepting- Pieter Spinder and Valentine Giraud.
- Organization 3.0 - Edwin de Bree
  Instead of telling people what to do (1.0), or activating people (2.0), people will act themselves (3.0).
- Business model canvas – Boukje Vastbinder
  A strategic management and entrepreneurial tool, it allows you to describe, design, challenge, invent, and pivot your business.
- Getting things done – Alex Falk
  Actionable, focus-driven tips, tricks and tools.
- Value-driven business in real life – Fokke Wijstra
  The role of values in larger organizations, and where to place focus.
- Bookkeeping – Geert Leijen
  The whats, whys, and hows of bookkeeping.
- Startup wheel – Pieter Spinder
  A simple, visual, and practical tool for business development.
- Sales – Wim Vrolijk
  Making sure we sell our products as well as services.
- Presentation skills – Henk Heikoop
  Improving presentation and speaking skills.
- Welcome rituals and more – Edgard Gouveia
  From the favelas of Brazil: The importance of play and joy while starting and working on projects.

PERSONAL LEADERSHIP
Change starts within yourself

- Journey and nature quest, The Heroes Journey – Martin Cadee
  Seeking wisdom from nature, away from society as we know it, and connecting through nature to the planet, ourselves, and the people around us.
- Nonviolent communication – Yoram Mosenzon
  An approach to communication based on compassion.
- The power of your voice – Carolien Borgers and Carianne Vermaak
  How do I use my voice, what more can I do, or what can I do differently to attract attention?

- New way of learning (1) – Thieu Besselink
- New way of learning (2) – Pieter Spinder
  Using the Petcha Kutcha method instead of a typical PowerPoint presentation.
- Herotalks and live storytelling – Guido Crolla
- Inspiration sessions - Martijn van Osch
  How to inspire ourselves and others: The power of storytelling.
- To hell with money – Charlie Davies de Mornay
  What is money, what does it do to us, and how do I behave with or without money?
- Mindfulness – Mirjam Spijker
  A mediation form in which one is aware (in a non-reactive way) of one's physical and mental states.
- Hero talk – Piet Hurkmans
- What makes you cry, die, or fly – Gil Alon
  How to be in touch with your inner self, focus on your intuition, and your relations with theater and music.
- Smart and sexy – Lisa Portengen
  A workshop on how to use your femininity (for women only).

BODY MOVEMENT
Move your butt

- Biodanza – Merijn Oudheusden
  Biodanza is a system of self-development that uses music, movement, and positive feelings to deepen self-awareness.
- Qigong and Kung Fu – Darryl Collett
  A qigong practice involves rhythmic breathing coordinated with slow stylized repetition of fluid movement, a calm state, and visualization of guiding qi through the body.
- 5-rhythms – Mirjam van Hasselt
  Movement meditation that draws from

indigenous traditions using shamanistic, ecstatic, mystical and, Eastern philosophies.

- Tai Chi – Tsi-La Piran
  Tai Chi is a Chinese martial art recognized for both its defense training and health benefits.
- Aikido - Huib Kraayenfeld.
  Aikido is a Japanese martial art which focuses not on punching or kicking opponents, but rather on using their own energy to gain control of them or to throw them away from you.

SOCIAL INNOVATION AND SUSTAINABILITY
Current problems in society and our environment - heroes and best practices

- Oasis Game – Niels Koldewijn
  Creating a better community via play and action. It started in Brazil, and is now exported to Europe.
- Sustainability in action – Godert van Hardenbroek
  Hands-on actions on what we can do now, and promises made by the participants.
- Sustainability – Ynzo van Zanten
  What is the state of the world on a big scale (think like Al Gore), and what are simple ideas that we can implement now?
- "Oh the meaning of it all" – Floris Koot, Valentine Giraud and Jord Hilstra.
  Personal reflections on the state of the world by Knowmads Business School facilitators.
- Cradle to cradle – Hanka Mouser
  Remaking the way we make things: A transformation of human industry via ecological design.

PROCESS AND PROJECT DESIGN

Group facilitation, understanding of group dynamics, diversity, decision-making, team play: Taking your own projects further

- Visual harvesting with Modelminds and visual thinking – Manuel Sturm and Oscar Westra van Holte
  Optimizing business meetings, and visualizing ideas and discussions.
- Deep democracy – Moraan Gilad
  A decision-making tool which strives toward a 100% buy-in from the group instead of 50%+1 vote; inspired by post-apartheid South Africa.
- Chaordic Stepping Stones – Arjen Bos, Kim van Rijt and Valentine Giraud
  The Chaordic Stepping Stones is a framework that can guide the development of a project, from its inception to its realization, harnessing the creative and innovative energy that lies between chaos and order.
- Value-based working – Fokke Wijnstra
  Fokke has 35 years experience in leading and motivating people and organizations. Increasingly, he focuses his work on organizing in complex environments.
- Client contact deadlines and love is the killer app – Pieter Kuijpers
- On culture – Roelijn Kok
  Working with diverse groups and how different cultures influence us and our work.
- Art of facilitation – Floris Koot and Tsi-la Piran
  How does one lead a process, what's the role of the participants, and how does the facilitator influence and use the group?
- How to facilitate groups – Doris Gottlieb
  How to lead a process, work with scepticism,

involve all participants, and put people in action.

- Project management movie – Pieter Spinder
  An intense day of work, full of deadlines, objectives, cooperation under stress, and reflection on what has happened.
- Walk out, walk on – Debbie Frieze and Tatiana Glad
- Theory U, YoU process, grounding insights into action – Joris Martens
  Otto Scharmer's Theory U is a change management method that targets leadership as a process of inner knowing and social innovation.

MARKETING AND CREATIVITY

Bringing yourself and your ideas into the world

- Creativity and brainstorming – Marcel Jongsma and Wicher Schols
  How does one brainstorm and make full use of their creative potential?
- Identity marketing – Ron van Gils
  What is a brand, what is your brand, and how can they be improved?
- Creativity and Storytelling – Marcel Kampman
- On creativity – Floris Koot
  Using the talking head methodology, the double diamond brainstorming tool, and more.
- Social media - Danny Koopman
  How to optimize your use of Facebook, Twitter, Linkedin, etc.
- Knowmads marketing – Pieter Spinder, Alex Falk and Guus Wink
  What is the Knowmads Business School story, and how to put this in action?
- Telling the Knowmads story – Niels Willems
  Six different approaches to the Knowmads

Business School story, from which almost all people can at least identify with at least one of them.

- Storytelling – Pieter Spinder
  Where do we find stories? How do you construct them? How do you share them? And, when do people listen?
- Video workshop – Guido Crolla and Duy vu Dinh
  How do you make a movie, including storyboarding, use of music, editing, etc.?

Thank you!

We would like to express our gratitude to the people (and organizations) that inspired us, helped improve this work, shared our messages with others, and asked difficult questions when necessary. In particular, we would like to thank: Ignaz Anderson, Teemu Arina, Ad Baan, Tomáš Biroš, Claire Boonstra, Ton van der Borg, Greg Braden, Martin Cadee, Gal Charu Weiler, Guido Crolla, Hans Erdmann, Michal Fabian, Alex 'Danger' Falk, Daniel Greenberg, Philippe Greier, Arthur Harkins, Peter Hartkamp, Jord Hilstra, Michelle Holliday, Pekka Ihanainen, Eva Janebová, Joseph Jaworski, Lois Josefson, De Kampanje Sudbury School, Marcel Kampman, KaosPilots Netherlands Teams 1 & 2, Knowmads Tribes 1-6, De Koers Sudbury School, Floris Koot, Peter Linde, Jacqueline Lindemulder, Mélanie Mercuri, John G. & Susan Moravec, Sébastien Paquet, Tsi-la Piran, Jana Procházková, Salima Punjani, Kim van Rijt, Martin Rodriguez, Mimsy Sadofski, Nikolaj Sahlstroem, Meïra Shalev, Ruti Shalev, Alexandre Spaeth, Jelte Spinder, Selma Steenhuisen, Vincent van der Veen, Carianne Vermaak, Ann Werner, Herman Wijfels, Niels Willems, Guus Wink, and Paul Zenke.

Special thanks are in order for Jaap Bijl, WDM stakeholder, for his courage to make the shift to organizing toward the '3.0' knowmadic way, and to Fokke Wijnstra from Finext for sharing his wisdom and experience.

We are also thankful for the contributions of Seats2Meet.com toward the production of the Knowmad Society iOS app, and also for their support in launching the book in Utrecht in December 2012. Particular thanks go to Mariëlle Sijgers, Ronald van den Hoff, Vincent Ariens, Raoul Wijnberg, and Nancy Meijer for their (continuing!) support.

Cristóbal Cobo's chapter was supported through the Knetworks project (Knowledge Dissemination Network for the Atlantic Area), and in collaboration with the Oxford Internet Institute.

Finally, this printed edition would be nowhere as lovely without the remarkable design work by Martine Eyzenga and Symen Veenstra.

COLOPHON

Knowmad Society

Edited by John W. Moravec. **Chapters** authored by by Thieu Besselink, Edwin de Bree, Cristóbal Cobo, Christel Hartkamp, Ronald van den Hoff, John W. Moravec, Christine Renaud, Pieter Spinder, and Bianca Stokman. **Afterword** by Gary Hart.

Book design by Martine Eyzenga (www.diezijnvaardig.nl). **Cover design** by Symen Veenstra (www.enkeling.nl). **Photographic images** are used with permission from the Knowmads Business School (www.knowmads.nl), Seats2Meet.com, and Maurice Mikkers (www.mauricemikkers.nl). **Figure 4** is based on public domain artwork created by palomaironique.

Published by Education Futures LLC, Minneapolis, Minnesota www.educationfutures.com

iOS application and other in kind resources provided by Seats2Meet.com

Portions translated and adapted from Cobo, C., & Moravec, J. W. (2011). *Aprendizaje invisible: Hacia una nueva ecología de la educación.* Barcelona: Laboratori de Mitjans Interactius / Publicacions i Edicions de la Universitat de Barcelona. (Under Creative Commons license.)

How to cite this book:
Moravec, J. W. (Ed.). (2013). *Knowmad Society.* Minneapolis: Education Futures.

ISBN (print edition): 978-0615742090
Copyright © 2013 Education Futures LLC

Made in the USA
San Bernardino, CA
17 February 2014